Planning and Politics


*For Patricia*

## Political and Economic Planning

COMMONWEALTH PREFERENCE IN THE UNITED KINGDOM
A Report

EUROPEAN ADVANCED TECHNOLOGY
A Programme for Integration
*by Christopher Layton*

EUROPEAN POLITICAL PARTIES
*Edited by Stanley Henig and John Pinder*

THE COMPANY
Law, Structure and Reform in Eleven Countries
*Edited by Charles de Hoghton*

THE MEMBER OF PARLIAMENT AND HIS INFORMATION
*by Anthony Barker and Michael Rush*
(Jointly with the Study of Parliament Group)

STATE ENTERPRISE: BUSINESS OR POLITICS?
*by David Combes*

WOMEN IN TOP JOBS
Four Studies in Achievement
*by Michael Fogarty, A. J. Allen, Isobel Allen and Patricia Walters*

THE CONTAINMENT OF URBAN ENGLAND
Urban and Metropolitan Growth Processes or Megalopolis Denied—*Volume One*
The Planning System: Objectives, Operations, Impacts—*Volume Two*
*by Peter Hall, with Ray Thomas, Harry Gracey and Roy Drewett*
(Now available as a one-volume paperback)

THE HOUSE OF COMMONS: SERVICES AND FACILITIES
*Edited by Michael Rush and Malcolm Shaw*
(Jointly with the Study of Parliament Group)

PARLIAMENTARY SCRUTINY OF GOVERNMENT BILLS
*by J. A. G. Griffith*
(Jointly with the Study of Parliament Group)

THE LOCAL GOVERNMENT ACT 1972: PROBLEMS OF IMPLEMENTATION
*by Peter G. Richards*

THE POWER OF THE PURSE
The Role of European Parliaments in Budgetary Decisions
*by David Combes et al*

INNOVATION AND PRODUCTIVITY UNDER NATIONALISATION
The First Thirty Years
*by Chris Harlow*

# Planning and Politics

*The British Experience 1960-1976*

MICHAEL SHANKS

Political and Economic Planning
George Allen & Unwin

By the same author

*The Stagnant Society*
*The Innovators*
*The Quest for Growth*
*European Social Policy, Today and Tomorrow*
*What's Wrong With The Modern World*
*Britain and the New Europe* (*with John Lambert*)
*The Lessons of Public Enterprise* (*ed.*)

First published in 1977

ISBN 0 04 330283 1 hardback
     0 04 330284 X paperback

George Allen & Unwin (Publishers) Ltd
Ruskin House, Museum Street, London WC1A 1LU

Political and Economic Planning
12 Upper Belgrave Street, London SW1X 8BB

Photoset in 10 on 11 point English Times by
Red Lion Setters, Holborn, London
Printed in Great Britain by
Biddles Ltd, Martyr Road, Guildford, Surrey

## Foreword
by Sir Montague Finniston

In few areas of human endeavour throughout the world has change been more evident in recent years than in the effort devoted to the planned operation of national economies. The need for change is easily recognised when traditional or existing practices can no longer sustain or support the circumstances of the time. In such situations, which are generally complex, matters if they take their own course generally do so for the worse; planning may do no better but at least it affords the possibility of improving on random anarchy (in the UK 'muddling through'). That this has been recognised by governments of all persuasions as a necessary feature of political life, is heartening.

Michael Shanks' book is a record of how the UK and its governments met the challenge of the years 1960-76. It is a record of trials (which can be creditable in a changing society); of errors (which are to be expected); and of personal arbitrariness (which is unforgivable). However good politicians may be at politics, political expertise does not augur success in planning, particularly when the end is apparently being treated as less important than the means. Perhaps greater humility, deeper thought, greater political and departmental selflessness, concentration on broader planning directives and lesser attention to the details of implementation, greater involvement of the working population and lesser intervention by Whitehall, could have avoided the perturbations in the country's economic activities during the 1960s and 1970s.

The lessons to be learned for national planning are that it takes time to think about what is needed; it takes time to organise plans and it takes time to implement plans; and the time for all these is greater than the life of single governments. Above all, plans are not immutable and planning must involve those who will be expected to achieve the plan when it is agreed.

I was a member of the NEDC when the current industrial strategy exercise was launched at Chequers in November 1975. It is an encouraging feature of this exercise that a conscious effort is being made to embody in it the lessons of previous attempts at national planning.

Michael Shanks' career has spanned the British and European scenes, government, industry and the academic world. With this wealth of background and since he himself participated in and experienced some of the events in the period under review, there can be few better qualified to have undertaken this task.

The personal recollections of politicians may be more attractive and more entertaining than this book. It is to be hoped, however, that politicians, planners and the public whose lives will be affected by future national plans, will read this account of past British experience if only to ensure that we do not re-enact the sad economic history of the country from 1960 to 1976.

March 1977

# Preface

This book appears under the joint sponsorship of the National Economic Development Office (NEDO) and Political and Economic Planning (PEP). They asked me to write an objective and analytical account of the various experiments in planning carried out in the United Kingdom, from the establishment of the NEDO in 1961 to the industrial strategy exercise of 1976, seeking to draw some lessons therefrom as to how our affairs might be better conducted in future. I was very honoured to be asked to undertake so challenging an assignment, especially as I was personally involved at various stages of the planning experiments during the last fifteen years. (I have tried not to let my personal experiences in any way influence my judgements of events and people, and where I have an interest to declare I have tried to explain this in the text.)

In writing the four historical chapters I have had the continual assistance of Sir Ronald McIntosh and his colleagues in the NEDO, and of John Pinder at PEP. They have both read the text, as have Sir Monty Finniston and T. C. Fraser, and I am indebted to all four for some invaluable comments and insights. I am also extremely grateful to many very busy people, including a number of former and present Cabinet ministers, previous director-generals of the NEDO and CBI, members of the TUC General Council, leading industrialists, bankers and civil servants, and members of the NEDO staff, who gave generously of their time in helping me to piece together and understand the past, and to form a view of the future. It would take too long to list them all, and it would be invidious to pick out any for special mention. It would also be unfair to saddle any of them—those whom I interviewed, and those who read the text, or both—with any of the errors of fact or interpretation which I am sure still exist despite their efforts, and for which of course I alone bear responsibility. It is the more important to stress this, since, despite the fact that my book was partly sponsored by the NEDO, at no time was there any suggestion that I would not be entirely free to give my own interpretation of the facts and my own view of what should happen in the future. That undertaking, which was a condition for my taking on the job, has been scrupulously adhered to throughout.

One of the problems about writing 'instant history' is that between the writing of a book and its publication much will have happened to influence and alter one's subject matter. There is no way round this problem, except to recognise it frankly. What I have tried to do in this book is to break the historical narrative, at the end of Chapter 4, in the summer holiday period of 1976, when the first phase of work on the industrial strategy was completed—and when the bulk of the text was in fact written. An attempt to assess the lessons of the fifteen years as a whole is made in Chapter 5, which inevitably looks towards the future. But already, in the brief period between August and November 1976 (when this Preface is being written), one's perspective has perforce been affected by the worsening economic picture. An attempt is made to bring the situation up to date and reflect on the immediate options and prospects for Britain in the Introduction, which follows this Preface. For the Introduction to postdate the text is no more illogical than many of the things which have passed under the name of planning or economic strategy in postwar Britain!

In writing this book I had the advantage of being able to draw on an unpublished history of the NEDC up to 1970 prepared for the Office by Michael Rothwell. I was also able to draw on some internal analyses made by the NEDO for the Council on the various planning exercises. Edited versions of these analyses appear as Appendices 1 to 6.

It would be ungenerous not to include, among those to whom one owes gratitude, one's own family. A husband and father in the throes of literary creation is not an attractive object to those near and dear to him. He continues to demand food and creature comforts. But in return he gives little, for his thoughts are too often elsewhere, with his Muse (or whatever name she is called by these days). Only the pounding of a typewriter reminds the author's family of his continued presence among them. To my wife and children, therefore, my eternal thanks for their tolerance and understanding—as indeed for all the other blessings their presence brings.

M.J.S.

# Contents

# Acknowledgement

Appendix 7 *An Approach to Industrial Strategy* (Cmnd 6315) is reproduced by permission of the Controller of Her Majesty's Stationery Office.

# Introduction

When I told friends that I was writing a book on Britain's experience of economic planning over the past fifteen years, the reaction of most was to look blank and ask: 'What planning?' The reaction is only marginally unfair. Considered objectively, Britain does not give the appearance of a country which has clearly thought out its future and evolved a strategy, or even one which has striven hard—except intermittently, to resolve an immediate crisis—to establish a consensus around which a strategy can be built. Parliament has almost totally failed to give a lead, and if it now feels itself bypassed by other bodies it really has nobody to blame but itself. But the other bodies also have not been terribly successful at subordinating sectional interests to the national good.

At the time of writing, in the autumn of 1976, the nation is in a battered and apprehensive frame of mind. Gone are the comforting illusions which have sustained us through so many years of disappointment and decline. If we can avoid the temptation to panic, or to sink into despair, this is not a bad climate in which to start seriously to plan. Plans must be based on realism, and realism is, for once in modern Britain, in season.

Moreover, the government has enunciated a strategy which commands a wide measure of agreement, at least in principle, among almost all sections of the nation. It is that in the next upswing of the business cycle priority must be given to exports and to capital investment in the private sector, at the cost of private consumption and public expenditure. At the same time, in the so-called 'industrial strategy' (see Chapter 4), the nation has a series of separate strategic exercises at the micro-economic level of individual industries and sectors, prepared by a series of sector working parties under the umbrella of the NEDC. What is missing is a national framework of medium-term macro-economic forecasts to link together the sector exercises and to quantify the national export-and-investment-first strategy. Also missing to date are the government measures which would ensure a higher rate of exports and investments.

So we are still at the stage of good intentions, in a situation where external constraints give the government little room for manoeuvre. In considering the next steps, it is important to bear in mind the state of public opinion. There is a greater sense of realism abroad, yes. But at the same time the failures of the past decade-and-a-half have left a residue of cynicism and suspicion which will be quick to spy and deride further errors.

In these circumstances it would be courting disaster to build a new grandiose structure like the National Plan (see Chapter 2). Rather, we should proceed to build on the 'bottom-up' basis of the industrial strategy exercise. That strategy has to be checked, tested and refined over the next eighteen months. At the same time, we have to move the exercise on from the examination of short-term constraints to that of medium-term growth; and here it will be important, I believe, to establish a credible link between the macro-economic framework and the micro-economic work of the sector working parties—supplemented no doubt in some cases by individual planning agreements.

The link is important, if only because one of the major constraints to medium-term growth is the low rate of capital investment in British industry. This is easily explicable if one considers that after making allowance for inflation the manufacturing sector has had cash flow deficits in five out of the last six years, and one of the great truisms of the business world is that 'you can't invest a deficit'. However, as business picks up, the readiness to invest will return, provided that businessmen have some confidence in the future. One way of meeting their hesitations is to provide a credible medium-term forecast for the growth of the economy, to which the government (and hopefully, though it may be a forlorn hope, the Opposition) is committed.

The other hurdle which will have to be overcome during 1977 is the negotiation of the next stage (Stage 3) of the counter-inflation policy. Another wage explosion in the upswing phase of the business cycle would be disastrous; but it will not be easy to avoid. The combination of requirements which will have to be met by Stage 3 is not easy: on the one hand, continuing restraint on wages, which will require some continuing controls on prices and profits; on the other, the opportunity for efficient firms to earn enough profits to enable them to invest adequately for the future; and enough flexibility in the wages policy to reward productivity, and to restore adequate differentials and incentives to higher-paid workers and particularly to supervisors, lower and middle management—a class which feels itself today squeezed between the twin forces of capital and labour. Time will be needed to negotiate a policy which provides adequate barriers against inflation while meeting the long-term needs of productivity, investment and personal motivation. So the negotiations will need to start early. On their outcome could depend the viability of any strategy for national survival and growth.

So much for the critical issues of 1977. Looking a little farther ahead, I believe we should seek to align our planning structures and our thinking on those organisations—particularly large corporations—which have a long and reasonably successful experience of planning. We should establish clearly what are our national objectives for the period ahead. These should be debated in Parliament as well as in NEDC and other relevant fora, and if possible they should secure at least a measure of inter-party assent, so that those who have to take decisions within the planning framework can judge for themselves what is likely to happen if there is a change of government during the plan's lifetime.

Clearly, the objectives must relate to the problems we face—a declining economy accompanied more recently by a measure of social ferment. We have to restore our balance of payments, reduce unemployment to tolerable dimensions, reverse the decline in our industrial structure and provide for a pattern of rewards and social improvements which we can afford and which will be accepted as in some sense corresponding to the requirements of justice and efficiency. Clearly we will have to establish trade-offs between these objectives, since the mere enunciation of them will carry little credibility after the disappointments of the past.

Within this framework of objectives, and a candid assessment of our strengths and weaknesses, and the major threats and opportunities facing us during the plan period, a quantified path can be traced, with alternative strategies to meet possible hypotheses. In this exercise rhetoric must be eschewed, and realism dominate. The scenario may not offer glittering prospects, but at least it should provide a set of parameters against which all the decision takers whose fortunes depend in greater or lesser degree on the performance of our economy can base their actions. And that is something which we have hitherto conspicuously lacked.

There are those who say that such planning, however desirable, cannot in practice be carried out publicly. Any nation, they say, has the choice between carrying out its planning processes in private, in which case discussion can be entirely frank and the planners can directly influence government decision making, but without having any direct impact on the nation at large; or in public, in which case the national debate is enriched but the planners are unlikely directly to influence government policy. Planning in government is secret but influential; 'open' or 'public' planning risks becoming a form of rhetoric.

Plainly there is a kind of choice here, but I believe it is one to be avoided. In the past in the UK, as I attempt to describe in Chapter 5, we have seemed at times to be operating both types of planning simultaneously, with the two main agencies—the Treasury and Neddy—not in full mutual communication. That is the worst combination, for it wastes time and breeds confusion. To have a planning system which operates close to the top of government but which is also open in the Neddy sense is a very difficult combination, but it can work, as I believe the French experience has shown—provided the planners are flexible and prepared to admit mistakes publicly.

It is possible that for the full achievement of such a structure in Britain we need another institution to complement the planning systems in Whitehall (centred on the Treasury and the Cabinet Office 'think-tank') and Neddy: a body which can reflect on government strategy and long-term national objectives. Such a body could be either inside the government machine, but detached from day-to-day work, and with freedom to communicate its findings from time to time to the outside world; or it could be an independent body with privileged access to Whitehall, which could be used by government for advice on the relationship of individual policies to agreed goals.

But, important as I believe these issues are, the immediate here-and-now need is the down-to-earth one of getting the country back from the brink of the abyss on which it has been teetering, on to a survival course. For that we need above all sobriety and a willingness to work hard. We need a government which, having mapped out a programme, sticks to it, and does not try to change the rules too often. We need trade unions and businessmen who will be prepared to stop blaming each other for the ills of the nation, and work hard together to put things right. We need a public which accepts that nobody owes the British a living, that miracles do not occur with great frequency, and that if we are not as rich or as powerful or as respected as we used to be, it is our own fault. In short, we need to heed the stern message on the clock of the old church tower at Furneux Pelham, in Hertfordshire: 'Time flies. Mind your business.'

# 1 1960-1964: Planning Under the Conservatives

Britain entered the 1960s in a mood of bewilderment and apprehension. The first postwar decade, from 1945 to 1955, had been one of relative economic success. True, the country was paying a heavy price for trying to maintain the pound sterling as an international reserve currency through the mechanism of the sterling area[1]; and it was becoming increasingly clear that our overseas defence expenditure—notably the cost of maintaining a major presence east of Suez—was further taxing our economic strength. The period had seen a succession of sterling crises, brought on by the overwhelming strength in the early postwar years of the US dollar.

At the same time, the reconstruction of British industry after the devastation and dislocation of the war seemed on the face of it to be going well. The tight system of wartime controls which had served so well in 1939-45 was gradually whittled down under the 1945-51 Labour Government, and much faster after 1951 when the Conservatives were returned to power under the slogan 'Set the people free'. Relations between the Trades Union Congress (TUC) and successive governments were good, and until the mid-fifties the UK was not significantly troubled by major labour disputes, as it was to be later on. And, if the British economy faced problems of external competitiveness and financial weakness in the decade after 1945, the same was true of all our major competitors outside North America.

It was after the second Conservative election victory of 1955 that doubts began to set in. The Conservatives had regained power in 1951 at the height of the Korean War inflation and a balance-of-payments crisis caused by soaring world commodity prices and an expanded defence programme. In 1952 the country experienced its first postwar recession, but it was relatively short-lived and recovery in 1953 was followed by boom years in 1954 and 1955. But the 1955 boom brought a renewed balance-of-payments crisis and once again, as in 1952, the Government put the brakes on the economy and induced another recession. The cycle was to be repeated exactly in the late 1950s: relative stagnation in 1956 and 1957, recovery at the end of 1958, boom in 1959 (accompanied by a summer of unprecedented sunshine, and leading to a third successive

Tory election victory), and another balance-of-payments crisis necessitating restrictive government economic measures in 1960-1.

The cumulative effects of this cycle—the so-called 'stop-go-stop' phenomenon—on business investment, and thus on long-term economic growth, were beginning to become apparent, and to enter into the currency of economic and political debate during the second half of the 1950s. After 1955 it became increasingly evident that growth rates in the British economy, and therefore in the nation's real standard of living, were falling behind those of all our major competitors except the USA, whose absolute standard of course was much higher (nevertheless, in the 1960s we were to lose ground to the USA too). Germany, Japan, France, Italy—not to mention our smaller overseas competitors—all were achieving growth rates, year in year out, which were double or more the British rate.[2]

Other things also began to shake British confidence and complacency after 1955. Our major Continental competitors came together to create a Common Market from which we excluded ourselves (the Foreign Office advised that they would never reach agreement); when the Market was established, we sought to link ourselves to it through the mechanism of a European Free Trade Area, and were rebuffed in somewhat cavalier fashion. Britain was clearly no longer the unquestioned 'top dog' in Western Europe, as she had been in 1945. The national humiliation was compounded by the disastrous Suez adventure in 1956, which cruelly exposed the limits of Britain's military and political power outside Western Europe. And on the home front too, the long honeymoon between the trade unions and the political establishment came to an end with a series of crippling strikes in the docks, on the railways, and in engineering and shipbuilding. The image of Britain as a country of civilised labour relations disappeared almost overnight as a generation of TUC 'elder statesmen' left the scene, some to be replaced by more militant younger men, others leaving behind union structures in considerable internal disarray. The British working man was becoming restive at the slow growth in his living standards and fluctuations in employment. In the next few years wage increases substantially in excess of productivity were forced out of reluctant employers and government.

All these discontents came to a head in 1960. The Conservatives had stuck constantly through the 1950s to a *laissez-faire* economic policy, in contrast to the *dirigisme* of their opponents. Economic argument tended to be conducted in somewhat *simpliste* terms of contrast between 'freedom' and 'controls'. But in 1960, confronted with the evident failure of 'freedom' to meet our national aspirations, and the obvious unattractiveness of a return to the rigours of the controlled economy, people began to ask themselves whether there was not a third alternative. And they thought they saw the glimmerings of such an alternative across the Channel, in the form of French indicative planning.

THE GLEAM ACROSS THE CHANNEL

Of all the economic 'miracles' which took place in the 1950s it was the French which perhaps surprised and intrigued the British most. In the case of Germany, Japan and Italy one could call in aid the psychological trauma of defeat as an explanation. Besides, it was well known that the Germans were hard and efficient workers, and that Italy enjoyed cheap labour, while Japan was a far-away country about which we understood little. But France? This was a country we had learned to patronise and despise in a friendly way during the interwar and war years; in the early postwar years the political instability of the Fourth Republic, with its succession of short-lived governments, gave the British no cause to revise their opinion of their charming but wayward neighbour. Yet in the late fifties it became clear that France, too, was demonstrably outstripping Britain's economic performance.

France's secret weapon appeared to be a sophisticated system of economic planning which established growth targets and objectives, helped to steer investment into the right quarters, allocated resources in an optimal way and, by showing business men the growth opportunities, stimulated a faster rate of investment in the private as well as the public sector. And, it was all apparently done by logic and persuasion, without controls or direction. It is small wonder that British businessmen, politicians, civil servants and academics, searching for a way out of the maze, should have fastened on the French planning system as a guide and inspiration, which might with luck and skill be adapted to meet the very different British institutional climate.

During 1960 there were a good many private discussions between French planners and British would-be planners. I attended one of these myself. (PEP played an important part in this dialogue, and its book *Growth in the British Economy* (1960) was influential.) It was clear that the French system did not work in quite such a purely 'indicative' way in practice as in theory. True, the planners could not give orders, and anybody who so wished could disregard their suggestions. On the other ·hand, the French Government was far more ready than the British to discriminate between enterprises in the granting of cheap credit, government orders or planning permission. A substantially larger proportion of French business capital was purveyed through the state rather than the private capital market than was the case in the UK, and the state varied the cost and availability of its capital between firms at its own discretion. To ignore the recommendations of the planners therefore posed the risk of getting into the government's bad books, and this could substantially harm a French enterprise[3].

However, these niceties did not appear to invalidate the wisdom of drawing on French experience. In November 1960 the Federation of British Industries (FBI) called a special conference in Brighton to consider possible solutions to the economic crisis. One of the working groups proposed, and the conference as a whole endorsed, the idea that the government should place before the country an assessment of economic expectations and intentions over the next five years—a Five-Year Indicative Plan, in fact. The plan should be jointly discussed between government, employers and trade unions, in the hope of reaching a consensus on policy which would remove the existing uncertainties (and so provide a better climate for investment), and hopefully help to resolve the increasing conflict between the unions on the one hand and governments and employers on the other, over the distribution of an inadequate national income.

The Chancellor of the Exchequer, Mr (now Lord) Selwyn Lloyd, was receptive to the idea. But there were two major hurdles to overcome. The first was the political anathema formerly placed by the Conservatives on planning. In fact, the Chancellor's only two allies in the Cabinet at that time were Mr Macmillan and Lord Hailsham. But as Mr Macmillan happened to be Prime Minister, his vote counted for more than that of the majority of the Cabinet, since nobody's ideological objections were of such intensity as to lead them to threaten resignation.

The second hurdle was the reluctance of the Treasury and some other government departments to let planning pass out of the control of the ministerial machine. After all, the French *Commissariat Général du Plan* has always been attached to the office of the French Prime Minister, in the heart of government.

This question, whether planning should be a direct function of government as in France, or whether it should be a consensus activity involving business and the trade unions as in the Netherlands and Scandinavia or Austria, has as we shall see remained a live one in the UK for the last decade and a half, and is still unresolved. But the initial decision, for which Mr Selwyn Lloyd with the backing of Mr Macmillan was directly responsible, was unequivocal. It was to establish a new tripartite body, outside the government machine, jointly responsible to government, industry and the TUC, to carry out national economic planning on an indicative—i.e. non-coercive—basis. The reasons for this decision are important and illuminating, for they indicate straight away the different concepts behind British and French planning.

First, the decision to separate the planning system from Whitehall reflected the growing dissatisfaction of ministers, both sides of industry and a substantial body of informed opinion with the quality of the Treasury's economic advice. This was not so much a question of technical expertise as of policy priorities. Those who favoured planning, whether in or out of the government, saw it as a means of stepping up the growth rate. Rightly or wrongly, it was felt that the Treasury was less interested in economic growth than in other economic objectives—primarily the maintenance of the pound sterling as a stable international reserve currency. Whenever the two objectives had come into conflict during the 1950s the Treasury, backed by the Bank of England, had persuaded ministers to give priority to the second objective, putting the pound before the growth of the domestic economy. In a rather muddled and intuitive way, Selwyn Lloyd and his supporters were looking for an alternative source of advice and expertise which in a crisis might give expression to a wider range of options. France had systematically since 1945 put economic growth before currency stability in her scale of priorities, being prepared to face regular devaluations rather than impose austerity on her business community. Admittedly, France did not have the discipline of maintaining an international reserve currency, and her economy was less subject to world trade than ours—though of course it became more so after the establishment of the European Common Market. Nevertheless the conventional wisdom outside the City was that we too should be prepared if necessary to take risks with the external account in order to maintain growth.

In the chapters which follow we shall be able to trace the implications of this view, and the various institutional expedients to which it has given rise. But in 1960 the position appeared clear. The Treasury could not be trusted with responsibility for planning designed to assure a faster rate of growth; and there was no other Whitehall department to which this responsibility could be given over the head of the Treasury. *Ergo*, a new independent authority must be created.[4]

The second argument tending in the same direction was this. Unlike France, successive British governments had identified as one of the major problems facing the UK economy the need to keep the growth in incomes in line with what the country could afford—which meant, broadly speaking, in line with the growth in productivity. This required the co-operation of the trade unions, for statutory wage control was not only difficult to enforce but also contrary to the prevailing belief in 'economic freedom'. During the first fifteen postwar years various attempts at an agreed incomes policy were made by successive British governments. The one really successful experiment was in 1948-50, under the chancellorship of Sir Stafford Cripps. This period of voluntary wage restraint operated by the TUC might well have developed as did similar operations in the Netherlands and Sweden, had it not been for the imported inflation following the Korean War boom, which caused prices to soar to a point at which the unions could no longer (especially at a time of over-full employment) restrain their members. Subsequent attempts by Conservative ministers to restore a system of voluntary wage restraint were less successful.

Selwyn Lloyd's hope was that if the TUC could be brought in as a partner in economic planning aimed at faster growth, it would be possible to broaden the agenda to include incomes policy; indeed, the logical link between incomes restraint-economic viability-growth would soon become self-evident as the exercise proceeded, and a deal might be done between government and unions which would trade short-term wage restraint for longer-term real growth, which would demonstrably benefit everybody. Thus the planning body would also be a bargaining forum, discussing in broad terms the distribution of the national cake as well as means of expanding it. But for this dual purpose a government department would be inappropriate. It was necessary to involve the trade unions in the operation as co-equal partners on the Scandinavian model, so that they felt a responsibility for the whole operation—and politically this was expecially necessary for a Conservative Government, the traditional 'enemy' of the trade union movement. Once again, in the chapters ahead we shall have to trace the evolution of the interconnection between growth planning and incomes policy in the UK. What is important to note here, particularly in view of subsequent developments, is the clarity with which the relationship was viewed at the start of the planning experiment.

THE BIRTH OF 'NEDDY'

After a good deal of behind-the-scenes negotiations, on 25 July 1961 Selwyn Lloyd announced the establishment of a National Economic Development Council (NEDC), with its own staff under an independent director-general, Sir Robert Shone, to be located eventually in Millbank Tower, conveniently near but outside the centre of government in Whitehall. The Council initially had twenty members—three ministers (the Chancellor, Minister of Labour and President of the Board of Trade), six each from the TUC and the private sector of industry, two from the nationalised industries, two independent experts and the director-general. The TUC members were nominated by the General Council, the six industrialists were appointed by the Chancellor. In his statement to the Commons, Selwyn Lloyd said:

I will deal first with growth in the economy. The controversial matter of planning at once arises. I am not frightened of the word. One of the first things I did when appointed Chancellor was to ask for a plan of the programme for development and expenditure in the public sector for five years ahead ... I have thought about it a great deal since and discussed it with representatives of both sides of industry ... Developments in the economy as a whole are studied by a number of bodies ... I think the time has come for a better co-ordination of these various activities. I intend to discuss urgently with both sides of industry procedures for pulling together these various processes of consultation and forecasting with a view to better co-ordination of ideas and plans. I stated some time ago that I thought an annual increase of 3% in the gross national product was feasible, but only if we have a 6% annual expansion of exports. I want to discuss with both sides of industry the implications of this kind of target for the various sectors of the economy.

Later Selwyn Lloyd referred to the need to 'promote a greater sense of national purpose in the conduct of our economic policy'.
There then followed a six-month period of somewhat tortuous discus-

sions between the Chancellor and the TUC. It may seem surprising that the hesitations came from this side rather than from the employer organisations, given the consistent support for the idea of planning which the unions had expressed since the war. The reservations were partly political. The idea of the trade union movement going into partnership with a Tory Government offended many of the loyalists of the Labour movement. Second, there were doubts about the government's sincerity. The statement of 25 July had been made, somewhat incongruously, in the context of yet another announcement of restrictive economic measures to cope with yet another sterling crisis. Third, and perhaps most important, were the hidden reefs of incomes policy. The TUC was not ready for the kind of dialogue on incomes policy, leading to commitments, which Selwyn Lloyd saw as one of the main agenda items for the NEDC. And among the measures included in the 25 July package were limitations on wage increases to which the unions strongly objected.

In the course of the next six months the TUC's objections were gradually whittled away, and the first meeting of the NEDC took place with full union participation on 7 March 1962. But in the course of the preliminary negotiations the Chancellor had had to abandon the idea of including incomes policy among the basic agenda items of the Council. Instead, he set up a separate body, the National Incomes Commission (NIC), without trade union participation or support, to review incomes policy questions.[5] In his own mind, however, this was a stop-gap pending the time when the TUC would agree to the subject coming on the NEDC agenda.

At the first meeting Selwyn Lloyd defined the task of the NEDC as follows:

To examine the economic performance of the nation with particular concern for plans for the future in both the private and the public sectors of industry.

To consider what are the obstacles to quicker growth, what can be done to improve efficiency, and whether the best use is being made of our resources.

To seek agreement upon ways of improving economic performance, competitive power and efficiency, in other words to increase the rate of sound growth.

So far as I know, no attempt has been made in the intervening years to alter or modify these terms of reference. Lloyd added:

I have tried to make it clear from the beginning that I would not seek to exclude any subject from our discussions, and that I would not arrogate to ministers the right to fix the agenda. I do not want this to be a body which just listens to government decisions, and is merely asked for comment. I want it to have an important impact on government policy during the formative stage, and upon the economic life of the nation. I believe that it can.

## THE FIRST PLANNING DOCUMENTS

At its second meeting, in May 1962, Shone put before the Council a proposal for what was to become Britain's first-ever national plan. The plan—or feasibility study, as it originally was—to cover the period 1961-6, was to be based on an assumption of a 4% per annum increase in gross domestic product. Although originally intended as a basis for forecasting, the figure was rapidly translated by both politicians and public into a target. The Prime Minister, in his public utterances, played a significant part in this distortion.[6] Not for the last time in this story long-term planning was distorted to serve the interests of short-term political advantage.

Work on the NEDC Plan had just started when in July Selwyn Lloyd was dismissed from the government and the country acquired a new Chancellor and the NEDC a new chairman. Reginald Maudling had been opposed to the idea of planning, and the institution of the NEDC, when Selwyn Lloyd first proposed it in Cabinet. But, once installed, he proved to be the most responsive Chancellor that the NEDC has so far experienced. Less innovative in his ideas than his predecessor, he was far better at communicating them and winning acceptance for them. His inarticulateness—rare for a leading politician—was one of the reasons for Selwyn Lloyd's dismissal. The other was that the Prime Minister thought he was too slow in taking reflationary measures to cope with the 1962 recession.

One of the secrets of the Maudling-NEDC honeymoon is in fact precisely that his chancellorship—nostalgically regarded by old NEDC hands as the institution's golden age—was a period of economic upswing, when political advantage and the state of the business cycle worked strongly in favour of the 'growth' message. For the first time since 1945 the UK had a Prime Minister and Chancellor who were intellectually and temperamentally prepared to take risks with sterling in the interests of a 'dash for growth'. In order to stimulate the investment needed for a period of sustained growth Mr Maudling was prepared to see the balance of payments go into deficit and to borrow abroad. Thus 1963 and 1964 were years in which the whole emphasis of short-term economic policy was geared to expansion, and NEDC provided the intellectual justification and the long-term prospectus for such a strategy.

It was in this honeymoon period that the Council and the Office (NEDO) acquired a personality and a standing with public opinion, exemplified by the affectionate nickname 'Neddy' which quickly passed into common currency and persists to this day. The Office, or staff, was split into two sections—the Economic Division under Sir Donald MacDougall and the Industrial Division under Mr T. C. Fraser. The former was primarily concerned with the macro-economic projections for the Plan, the latter with the micro-economic implications for individual industrial sectors. Numbers at that stage were small—the Industrial Division consisted of only ten professional executive staff by the end of 1962. The two divisions worked closely together, the planning function helping to identify the obstacles to efficiency which the Industrial Division would need to deal with. The decision was taken during 1963 to set up a series of individual economic development committees (EDCs) for key industrial sectors, with the same tripartite structure as the Council, serviced by the NEDO, each with an independent chairman (normally an industrialist). These EDCs—promptly christened 'Little Neddies'—had the following terms of reference:

> Within the context of the work of the NEDC, and in accordance with such working arangements as may be determined from time to time between Council and the Committee, each committee will:
> (a) examine the economic performance, prospects and plans of the industry, and assess from time to time the industry's progress in relation to the national growth objectives, and provide information and forecasts to the Council on these matters;
> (b) consider ways of improving the industry's economic performance, competitive power and efficiency and formulate reports and recommendations on these matters as appropriate.

Thus the EDCs had both a planning role, in association with the Council, and an 'efficiency' role—analysing and hopefully providing solutions for the obstacles to growth encountered at 'micro' level—which as time went on was to become more and more autonomous and divorced from the Council. We shall trace this evolution in the chapters which follow.

This dual approach—on the one hand projecting a national economic growth path and assessing the implications, and on the other hand analysing the practical obstacles to faster growth within the industrial and social structure—was followed in the first 'Neddy' Plan, published in two stages in February and April 1963.

'GREEN' AND 'ORANGE' BOOKS

The first part—the so-called 'Green Book'—was entitled *Growth of the United Kingdom Economy to 1966*. [7] It set out in considerable detail the implications of a 4% per annum real growth in gross domestic product (GDP) in the five years 1961-6. At the national level this would require productivity to grow by 3.2% a year, industrial investment by 5.3% per annum, exports by 5.0% p.a. (compared to an existing rate of around 3%). Manpower could be expected to increase by 0.8% p.a.

These national projections were only a part of the exercise. The other, and in many ways more interesting, part reviewed the feasibility of this growth pattern by means of a dialogue carried out with seventeen major industrial sectors, in both the public and the private domain.[8]

The major findings of the industrial inquiry were that the seventeen sectors expected to increase their overall production by 4.8% p.a.; the rest of the economy would thus need to contribute 3.5%. For some—notably electricity and some parts of chemicals—this would require a very marked acceleration in investment. Others, such as steel and motor manufacture, by and large had adequate installed capacity, though there was scope in both cases for 'deepening' investment. Public building investment would rise sharply, and the proportion of national income saved would need to go up by 2% to finance the needed investment increase.

The most problematic aspect of the exercise was the big increase projected for exports, designed to turn a deficit of £77 million in the 1961 balance of payments into a £300 million surplus in 1966. This surplus was thought necessary to finance an expected net outflow of long-term government capital (£200 million) and private capital (£150 million), as well as assuring some improvement in the UK's net monetary position.

Consumption, both public and private, was expected to grow less than GDP—by around 3.5% p.a. in both cases—indicating a significant shift towards exports and investment. (Imports were anticipated to rise by 4.0% a year; the Plan assumed British entry into the Common Market before 1966.) Since population would be growing during the Plan period, the growth in consumption per head would be less—only 2.8% p.a. A measure of consumer restraint was therefore clearly implicit in the Plan, though how it was to be obtained was not stated.

The other major feature—the projected rise in productivity—could be justified a little more easily. With improving technology the underlying rate of productivity increase in the economy (a notional figure by which the Treasury set great store throughout the 1960s) had been steadily increasing; from an average of 2½% p.a. in the second half of the 1950s it was thought to have reached 3% in 1962. A further rise of 0.2% did not seem out of the question.

The Plan also had the advantage that the base year chosen, 1961, was a year of relatively low activity and under-used investment capacity (reflecting the results of the capital spending boom of 1959). On the other hand, exactly the same could be said of 1962, when the economy grew by only 2%. Thus the progress in the last four years would need to be proportionately greater.

The dialogue with the seventeen industrial sectors seemed to indicate that there was nothing in the Plan's projections which was inherently implausible, and no major inconsistencies were revealed (though this could have been due partly to lack of time in the planning process!). Inevitably the exercise was carried out in a great hurry, by people and organisations with very varying degrees of sophistication and awareness of what they were doing; and inevitably there were subtle pressures to 'make the figures add up'. One can make many criticisms at a technical level of the operation. Nevertheless, what the Plan showed was that it was perfectly possible to envisage a pattern of balanced growth which would add some £5.75 billion at 1961 prices to British GDP without causing intolerable strains, provided everybody concerned took the appropriate measures. What it did not do was to provide any assurance that such measures would be taken, or indicate any fall-back position were they not taken.

However, in a companion document—the so-called 'Orange Book', entitled *Conditions Favourable to Faster Growth*, published in April 1963—the NEDC did try to spell out the measures that would have to be taken to turn the UK from a stagnant to a growth economy.[9] As a summary of the 'ruin in the nation' the Orange Book makes salutary reading, and it is sad and instructive to re-read it today to see how many of its criticisms are still valid, despite the very considerable institutional changes which have taken place in many of the areas covered. The main subjects listed were the need to improve the role of education, management education and training in the cause of economic growth; measures needed to promote mobility and ease the pains of redundancy; the necessity of an active regional policy; measures to strengthen the balance of payments; the role of taxation in assisting growth and efficiency; the implications of different levels of demand for growth (implications for output, investment, efficiency, structural change, prices and incomes, balance of payments); the need for price and cost competitiveness; and the necessity for government, management and trade unions to work together to achieve the growth objective.

The message of the Orange Book was clear. There was no necessary conflict between economic growth and other objectives, provided the right measures of structural reform were taken; and while the prime responsibility in most cases rested with government (since they involved changes in public policy or in public spending), if they were to succeed there must be co-operation from the other major interests in the community.

Ominously, by far the weakest section of the Orange Book was that dealing with incomes policy. It was clear that as yet there was no consensus on this subject among the NEDC membership. The other weak section, significantly, was that concerned with the balance of payments.

The Orange Book came out just in time for Mr Maudling's 1963 Budget; and it provided him with a blueprint for structural reform which he used to the full. Never again (at least until 1976) was the imprint of Neddy on economic policy to be so clearly seen. Unfortunately, these measures were combined with stimulus for a consumer spending boom which, at least in the short term, took resources away from exports and investment. It is also clear, in retrospect, that the Orange Book section on the balance of payments, which argued that payments difficulties encountered in the early stages of an investment boom should be met by borrowing rather than by throttling back investment needed for long-term growth and efficiency, was not only over-sanguine in tone (no doubt as a corrective to the deflationary bias in the Bank of England and parts of the Treasury), but was interpreted too optimistically by the politicians, who tended to ignore the warnings in Neddy's small print.

NEDDY RUNS INTO TROUBLE

When the NEDO reviewed progress on the Plan a year later, in *The Growth of the Economy* (March 1964),[10] it found that public sector capital spending had grown faster than indicated in the Plan; current expenditure was on target; education close to target; the road programme ahead of target; investment in electricity generation, gas and telecommunications had increased substantially; private industry's investment plans, though not growing so dramatically, had nevertheless evidently been scaled up (though how far this reflected belief in the wisdom of Neddy's projections, how far the normal optimism at the peak of the business cycle, is problematic). But on the balance of payments it said: 'A reassessment suggests that imports of both finished and semi-finished manufactured goods are likely to increase more rapidly than was estimated a year ago', and it spoke of the balance of payments as 'an area presenting particular difficulties'.

In short, under the NEDC's influence Mr Maudling seemed to have generated an oldfashioned consumer boom, heavily oriented towards construction and the consumer durables, which, far from strengthening exports, was sucking in imports. The question was whether this pattern would be reversed in time, as buoyant consumer orders generated new capital investment (the spare capacity identified in the Green Book had been used up remarkably quickly in the ensuing twelve months), and the new investment produced increased exports. Mr Maudling argued that time was needed for the 'dash for growth' to generate the needed structural shift in the economy. In the meantime the boom was having a remarkable effect on the fortunes of the Conservative Government, rocked by a series of misadventures during the recession period, and further shaken by the abrupt departure on grounds of health of Harold Macmillan in 1963, and his replacement as Prime Minister by the inexperienced (in the economic field) Sir Alec Douglas-Home (now Lord Home). The last thing his colleagues wanted of Mr Maudling was a further bout of 'stop-go-stop'.

Thus the boom went on, throughout 1963 and 1964, but with increasing signs of strain on the balance of payments, and the re-emergence of bottlenecks in some parts of the domestic economy.

In the meantime discussion at the NEDC began increasingly to focus on incomes policy. The Chancellor argued that the government had done all it could to implement the Council's findings, and it was now up to the other partners to do their bit. Once again, as the economy picked up, wages and salaries were starting to rise appreciably faster than output, thus endangering still further our competitive position. *The Growth of the Economy* dwelt on this aspect in sombre terms, implying that unless it was solved the growth experiment might have to be abandoned.

The problem was complicated by the fact that the NIC was being advised by the government's chief economic adviser that wage increases should be kept in the 2-2½% range, a line which greatly annoyed the TUC. There was regular discussion of incomes policy by NEDC throughout the summer and autumn of 1963, with the TUC members insisting that restraint on incomes must be accompanied by restraint on prices and profits, while the furthest the employers were prepared to go was a tax on profits. In January 1964 Mr Maudling tried to get agreement to a joint declaration of restraint on prices and incomes, but failed. This failure set a blight on the Council, which in effect continued until the October 1964 election. Little more of consequence, apart from the establishment of the first EDCs, emerged from Neddy during 1964.

In fact the Chancellor probably made his bid for an agreed incomes and prices policy a little too late. By the end of 1963 the recovery had proceeded to the point at which employers were themselves beginning to bid up the price of labour by offering 'above the odds' to secure increasingly scarce labour; and the volume of demand was such as to make price restraint an unattractive option. The top of a boom is not a good time to seek for agreed measures of restraint.

Moreover, the country was in a pre-election mood. It seemed very probable that an election would be held before the end of 1964. The new Leader of the Labour Party, Mr (now Sir) Harold Wilson, was projecting major institutional and structural reforms, and it was clear that the role of the NEDC would be drastically revised in the likely event of a Labour victory at the polls. This inevitably affected the attitude of the TUC, caught in a conflict of loyalties between commitment to Neddy and allegiance to the Labour movement. Meanwhile, as the 'dash for growth' continued, the Conservatives began to come up from behind in the opinion polls as pre-election fever mounted. It was an exciting period, but not one conducive to the calm long-term analysis which was the role of the NEDC.

NOTES

1  Members of the Sterling Area—largely, but by no means entirely, coterminous with the Commonwealth—held their currency reserves in the form of credits with the Bank of England, which they were normally entitled to draw at will. These were the so-called 'sterling balances'. From being a tightly knit entity in the early postwar years of dollar shortage, the Sterling Area bonds became progressively loosened during the 1950s and 1960s. After the Basle Agreement of 1968 (q.v. Chapter 3) the Sterling Area ceased to be a significant factor in British economic management, until the problem resurfaced after the oil price explosion of 1973, when Britain once again became a very large foreign debtor.

2  In the period 1949-59 annual gross domestic product rose by 7.4% in West Germany, 5.9% in Italy, 4.5% in France, 3.4% in Sweden and 2.4% in the UK. Of seventeen European countries, only Ireland had a lower growth rate than Britain.

3  For a further assessment of the 'French connection' see Chapter 5.

4  Writing in the Conservative journal *Crossbow* in August 1963, Selwyn Lloyd stated:
    'NEDC is much better outside the Whitehall complex, for it is much more likely to be

successful in bringing together the views of people inside and outside Government if it is independent. In addition, this independence gives its studies a value and authority which they would not have were the NEDC staff just another government department. Also, for NEDC to be effective, the representatives of the trade unions, private employers and the nationalised industries have to feel that their views do make an impact on the Government at the time when policy is at the formative stage. And one would expect that having once agreed on recommendations, the members of NEDC will feel, to some extent at least, committed to use what influence they have, to get them carried out.

5  Though planned and conceived by Selwyn Lloyd, the NIC was announced just after his departure from the Treasury.

6  Notably in a speech to a Conservative women's rally in the Albert Hall in May 1962, in which he said: 'With my full support the Council are using an ambitious target figure of 4% growth in the national product ... it is not a forecast; it is a target ... We are nailing our colours to the mast of expansion: a 22% increase by 1966.'

7  For a fuller analysis, see Appendix 1.

8  The seventeen were: coal, gas, electricity, Post Office, agriculture, chemicals, chocolate and sugar confectionery, construction, construction materials, heavy electrical machinery, electronics, iron and steel, machine tools, motor vehicles, paper and board, petroleum, wool textiles. Together they accounted for nearly half of industrial production, around 40% of national product and of employment, about the same proportion of exports and nearly half of total expenditure on fixed investment other than dwellings.

9  For a fuller analysis, see Appendix 2.

10  For a fuller analysis, see Appendix 3.

# 2 1964-1966: Labour's National Plan

The general election of October 1964 turned out to be a very close-run affair. Labour emerged with an overall majority of three. Harold Wilson took office as Prime Minister, but the nation was run in a kind of pre-election atmosphere until March 1966, when after going to the polls again Mr Wilson secured an overall majority of ninety-seven. The narrowness of Labour's majority, and the knowledge that a further election would therefore have to be held before long, is an essential element when considering what happened in the first Wilson administration.

A second factor to be borne in mind is that Labour's strategy had been largely drawn up in the recession period of 1962. It was therefore much more attuned to the achievement of growth than to coping with the actual situation which confronted it on coming to power—an economy at the top of a boom and verging on overheating, a balance-of-payments deficit of £769 million (a much more significant figure then than it would be today), and an international financial community extremely apprehensive over Labour's policy and on the verge of withdrawing confidence from sterling.

In these circumstances it is not surprising to find an element of ambivalence, not to say confusion, in Labour's economic policy in the early days. But this was further compounded by the major changes introduced into the structure of government.

The Labour Party shared, to an exaggerated degree, the suspicions of the Treasury and the Bank of England which had led their opponents to set up the NEDC. But for Labour the NEDC did not seem the right solution. Being outside the government machine, in their view, it inevitably lacked the knowledge and the power seriously to confront the Treasury. When the chips were down, it was bound to be relegated to the sidelines. It also offended against the strongly centralist tradition within the Labour administration. Having after thirteen frustrating years at last got its fingers—albeit somewhat tenuously—on the levers of power, the Labour Party did not relish the prospect of sharing this power with outside parties. And it was also concerned at the risk of ministers being given contradictory advice from two sets of advisers in such a delicate area as economic policy.

So Labour's solution was to take back the responsibility for economic planning and growth policies into Whitehall, and put it into a new ministry, the Department of Economic Affairs (DEA), whose minister, Mr (now Lord) George Brown, ranked second only to the Prime Minister in the Cabinet hierarchy, and above the Chancellor, Mr James Callaghan. Functions were transferred to the DEA, not only from the Treasury and Neddy, but also from other senior Whitehall departments, notably the Board of Trade. Not surprisingly it was an unpopular innovation.

The DEA's role was essentially to *get growth*, while the Treasury's role in the new structure was seen primarily as maintaining financial viability and managing the budget and public expenditure. (When the DEA's original blueprint was drawn up, by a small Fabian Society working group of which I was a member, we envisaged that *capital* expenditure in the public sector—a crucial element in national economic growth—would come under the DEA, while *current* public spending would remain the Treasury's responsibility. But this responsibility was traded away by George Brown and his permanent secretary in a meeting with their opposite numbers in the Treasury on the morrow of the Labour victory. I believe, for reasons which are set out below, that this contributed significantly to the subsequent impotence and demise of the DEA.)

### THE DEA—STRUCTURE AND FUNCTIONS

The new department was organised into four main sections. First, and largest, was the Economic Planning Division, which in fact consisted largely of the Economic Division from the NEDO, brought in *en masse* from Neddy under their head Sir Donald MacDougall. This division was given responsibility for preparing a new National Plan to replace the existing NEDC Plan—a plan which in this case would carry the full authority and commitment of government. One of Labour's major criticisms of the NEDC plans had been that they did not carry this commitment (somewhat ironic, in view of subsequent developments).

Working closely with the Economic Planning Division was a much smaller Industrial Policy Division, largely staffed by outsiders brought into government on a temporary secondment basis (of whom I was one). The task of this division was to take over responsibility for steering the work of the 'little Neddies' (EDCs), now nine in number (to rise to twenty-one by 1968), particularly as regards the 'efficiency' part of their mandate, and generally to explore ways of improving industrial performance. George Brown and his advisers had a wistfully naive belief that the EDCs, which were neither statutory nor representational bodies, could somehow be turned into important agents for industrial change.

The third division, the Economic Policy Division, had *inter alia* the all-important responsibility for achieving a prices and incomes policy. As we shall see, this was perhaps the most important element in the DEA's range of policies. The fourth division was concerned with regional policy, and here again Labour produced a constitutional innovation. It believed that the National Plan, unlike the Neddy plans, should have a regional dimension; and that, following the Orange Book, growth policies should be regionally oriented. To enable this to take place, regional economic planning councils consisting of independent people of local standing under an independent chairman were set up in each of the eight main English regions[1] as well as in Scotland, Wales and Northern Ireland; and the regional officers of the relevant Whitehall departments were formed into regional economic planning boards, under DEA chairmanship, to service the Planning Councils and to co-ordinate government regional policy. Given certain assumptions, this could have developed into an exciting concept of regional devolution. But, as we shall see, it was not to be.[2]

Such, then, was the structure of the DEA, Labour's chosen instrument for economic planning. Clearly in the new structure the role of Neddy was diminished. George Brown took the chair of the Council, and NEDC and NEDO were involved in the work of preparing the National Plan. But the function of the Council was seen essentially as consultative, while the Office staff, diminished in number, were really ancillary to the DEA officials (many of them their recent colleagues). Naturally, morale at Neddy was low.

For the EDCs on the other hand, and for the NEDO Industrial Division which serviced them, the perception from Whitehall was much more favourable. They were very much involved in the development of the National Plan, and the NEDO staff on the whole were able to work well in harness with the DEA industrial advisers, with whom in many cases they shared a common industrial background (and sometimes a common and reciprocated suspicion and lack of understanding of the regular civil servants from the Board of Trade and other 'sponsor' departments). During the period of the DEA a gulf began to develop between the NEDC, endlessly discussing broad problems of the macro-economy, and the EDCs, immersed in detailed micro-problems which they often found difficulty in communicating to the outside world (especially where there did not exist strong links with relevant trade associations)—and more concerned with their relationship to the relevant Whitehall departments than to the remote and seemingly ineffectual parent Council.

LABOUR'S GROWTH STRATEGY

If one looks at Labour's approach and compares it to that of the outgoing Tory administration, it is clear that both ardently desired 'sound, sustainable growth'. The Conservatives were more ready to take risks with the balance of payments to generate an expansionist mood in the economy; Labour was more interested in structural changes to enable resources to be used better. Hence Labour's concern to establish a viable prices and incomes policy, a better distribution of resources between the regions, and its greater readiness to intervene in questions of industrial structure and policy. This difference in approach not only reflected the divergent ideologies of the two parties. It could also be said to reflect, at least to some extent, the objective situations confronting them.

As we have seen, the Tory growth experiment started at a time of slack in the economy. By the time Labour took office that slack had disappeared, except for certain pockets of under-activity. Yet the economy had failed to 'take off'. After the sharp rise in output in 1963-4, by the beginning of 1965 output had levelled off at a high level of activity and employment, but with little sign of any breakthrough in productivity which would rid us of our excessive dependence on manufactured imports, or bring our output per man nearer to our major overseas competitors. The Conservatives could argue—and do, to this day—that more time was needed for the investment generated by the Maudling 'dash for growth' to come on stream, and for traditional restrictive attitudes on the part of management and men to be eroded. But from the Labour Government's point of view, the only way to convert a temporary upturn into 'sound, sustainable growth' in the absence of unused resources was to promote major structural changes to shift resources already in use from low-priority to high-priority sectors. That was the objective of the elaborate planning machinery installed by Labour, centred on (but not exclusive to) the DEA.

We shall never know whether the Tory hypothesis would have been proved right had the Maudling policy been maintained. What can be said, I think, is that Labour's concern to achieve structural changes in the economy was perfectly respectable, but that unfortunately the means chosen proved self-defeating.

The cardinal error was the attempt to divide the functions of economic management between the Treasury and the DEA, in such a way as to focus the interest of the Treasury on the short term and the DEA on the long term. The division was rigid. The Chancellor was no longer a member of the NEDC, and during the George Brown era no Treasury minister or civil servant took much interest in Neddy. This meant that decisions were taken on short-term policy grounds which had profound influences on long-term development, with the minimum of discussion. This was not just a matter of bad personal relations between the ministers concerned, and between their officials, but a reflection of the fact that within a political democracy the pressures of short-term survival are always likely to predominate in periods of crisis; and the mid-1960s were a period of almost continual economic crisis, the burden of solving which fell squarely on the Treasury. Thus, while in principle economic policy was handled by the triumvirate of Wilson, Brown and Callaghan, in fact as time went on it was progressively the Chancellor's view which triumphed. And the structure devised was such as to reinforce the

Treasury's traditional weaknesses: a low concern for growth among economic priorities, a lack of knowledge of and interest in the working of industry (including the impact on industry of fiscal and monetary policies), and an over-riding concern for the defence of sterling. Thus, as the balance of power within Whitehall tilted away from the DEA and towards the Treasury, the ills which Labour in Opposition had diagnosed and sought to cure became embedded deeper and deeper in the structure of government.

Not all of this became clear immediately. Labour's first attempts to grapple with the payments crisis did not do violence to the party's beliefs. There was an effort to deal directly with the overseas balance without depressing home demand, by a surcharge on imports (which proved extremely unpopular with our trading partners in the European Free Trade Association[3]—EFTA—and had soon to be abandoned), restraints on overseas investment, and more foreign borrowing. During 1965 and early 1966 the domestic economy remained buoyant, and despite a payments crisis in mid-1965 the overseas balance remained— albeit precariously—under control. But the hoped-for rise in productivity did not take place, the annual increase in the two years being only about 2½%. The economy was apparently jogging on much as it had done before.

But in fact the position had worsened considerably in the five years since 1960. For it was becoming increasingly obvious that the relative weakening of Britain's industrial structure relative to our competitors meant that the pound sterling was becoming overvalued in world markets. The exchange rate of the pound in relation to the dollar and other major currencies had not changed since the 30% devaluation carried out by Sir Stafford Cripps in 1949. But Britain's cost structure compared to others had deteriorated substantially—not because our internal costs and prices had risen faster than others in absolute terms, but because productivity had risen far less, and therefore costs per unit of output had risen more. The result was that in order to sell profitably abroad British exporters had to charge prices which were uncompetitive; or, alternatively, to win business they had to sell at prices which were much less remunerative than home sales. Thus, whenever home business was good, imports tended to be sucked in and home production diverted from exports to the home market.[4] The world could see clearly the weakening in Britain's competitiveness, and the effects of the structural shift in the economy away from exports towards home consumption, and concluded that sooner or later the pound would have to be devalued. It therefore became sensible to speculate against sterling, thus increasing its weakness and the strains on it.[5]

INSTRUMENTS OF INTERVENTION

There were a number of ways in which this structural imbalance could in theory be corrected. The Labour Government tried most of them during its first three years in office. One method would be to reduce costs in relation to our competitors by a policy of incomes control. Here Labour had at first more success than its predecessors. By the end of 1964 George Brown had persuaded the leaders of the employer organisations[6] and the TUC to sign a 'Declaration of Intent' establishing a voluntary policy for control of incomes and prices. Early in 1965 a new independent body, the National Board for Prices and Incomes (NBPI), was set up to replace the NIC, abolished on the morrow of Labour's election victory. The NBPI was headed by a former Conservative Cabinet minister, Mr (now Sir) Aubrey Jones. Its function was advisory, to investigate cases of income and/or price increases referred to it by government, to see whether in its view they were justified. Unlike its predecessors, it enjoyed TUC support, and acquired over the next few years considerable influence and prestige. Though prices and incomes negotiations were formally kept off the NEDC agenda, Aubrey Jones became a member of the Council, and the intention was to establish a progressively closer linkage between the management of economic growth and price and income restraint. The Neddy Office was asked to report periodically to the Council on the movement of incomes and prices.

George Brown invested an enormous amount of energy and political capital in securing an effective but voluntary prices and incomes policy and resisting proposals for statutory control which would have been unacceptable to the unions and extremely difficult to enforce at the top of a boom. So far as prices were concerned, the mechanism for effective controls such as had operated in wartime no longer existed in Whitehall, even had such a policy been deemed desirable.

On the other hand, while the NBPI had a considerable persuasive and educational influence (not always—as in the case of the nationalised industries—for the good), its role in actually keeping down prices and incomes is much harder to evaluate. It could only investigate cases referred to it by government; and its reports, when they appeared, were recommendations without statutory or legal force—at least in the private sector. Since there was no requirement on industry to notify the government of wage or price changes in advance, the Board's reports were necessarily *ex post facto*. At the beginning of 1966 the government sought to remedy this by putting on the statute book legislation requiring wage claims, and proposed price increases in a range of key industries, to be notified to it in advance, so that there would be an opportunity for prior investigation and decision whether or not to refer the increases to the NBPI before they took effect; this legislation would involve a temporary 'stop' on price and wage increases up to a possible maximum of four months, but no more. There was still no mechanism for actually forbidding or limiting wage or price rises at the end of the day.

Such restraining influence as the NBPI did have was more evident in the field of prices than of wages.[7] At the start of 1966 wages were rising at an annual rate of around 9%, prices by 5%, output by little more than 1%. Not only did this mean that our international competitiveness was being eroded. The fact that wages were rising much faster than prices meant that profits were shrinking while home market sales were buoyant. This acted as a disincentive to investment as well as to exports, thus working directly counter to the government's objectives on the restructuring of the economy.

Another way of tackling this structural imbalance was through direct action on the balance of payments, making exports cheaper and imports more expensive. Labour tried this by means of the import surcharge already referred to, by an export rebate scheme, by attempts to limit overseas private investment and by taking steps to reduce government defence spending east of Suez. Of these only the last—which was not to show its full effect until the end of the decade—was of lasting significance. The other measures were marginal. In any case the government's hands were somewhat tied as regards direct action on the balance of payments, because of its desire to join the European Economic Community (EEC)—an attempt which was in fact destined to be vetoed by the French President, General de Gaulle.[8]

A third method of attacking structural imbalance is through direct action in industry at the micro level, identifying the obstacles to efficiency and growth at sector, firm and plant level, and trying to remedy these directly, regardless of the overall macro-economic framework. Both the Labour Government and Neddy set great store by this approach. On the fiscal side, the government produced a whole raft of innovations, of which perhaps the most significant from this point of view was the replacement of investment allowances by direct cash grants.[9] The NEDC produced in 1965 a report on *Investment Appraisal*, recommending the use of discounted cash flow (DCF) techniques—perhaps the most influential of the very many technical publications produced by Neddy over the years. Progress was made on a number of the points identified in the NEDC Orange Book—on the development of management education, technical education, training and retraining facilities, and so on. The EDCs were stimulated to find ways of improving performance and productivity in their industries. A number of points emerged: the need for better co-ordination between makers and users in some industries; concentration on longer production runs in others; better use of public puchasing as a basis for standardisation, exports and the introduction of advanced technology; and many others.

The problem, however, was that while all this might be useful and stimulating to those firms represented on the EDCs, there were great difficulties in communicating their findings to those outside. Where an EDC was operating in a relatively oligopolistic industry with a strong trade association network (as in chemicals or electrical engineering, for example), this could be overcome; but by no means all industries fall into this convenient pattern. And, as already indicated, the EDCs had no authority to commit their industries to policies, still less to dictate to them. Their role was aptly described by NEDO's industrial director as 'to know and to enquire, to initiate and to prod, to advise and to seek to influence'.

One of the major obstacles to growth identified by governmental and Neddy studies in a number of cases was the actual structure of industry—the number and spread of firms. These studies concluded that in some cases the only way to achieve the economies of scale and rationalisation, the application of effective management and the establishment of a competitive base in world markets, was by mergers. The market economy, left to itself, might not promote such mergers quickly enough or in the right way. So in 1966 the government established a new institution, the Industrial Reorganisation Corporation (IRC), with an initial capital of £150 million, to promote mergers and rationalisation schemes in those sectors of British industry where they appeared plainly desirable. Its chairman, Sir Frank (now Lord) Kearton, was appointed to the NEDC. The IRC was to play a major role in a number of key restructuring exercises, for example the takeover of English Electric and AEI by GEC to create a single British electrical engineering giant, and the more controversial merger of Leyland and BMH to create the giant motor firm of British Leyland under Sir Donald (now Lord) Stokes.

A second major engine of intervention was the newly created Ministry of Technology, with responsibility for government research stations, the Atomic Energy Authority, the National Research and Development Council (NRDC), development contracts in private industry, and sponsorship functions in regard to industry's own research associations (which are partly government-financed) and for a small group of key industries—machine tools, computers, electronics and telecommunications. The purpose of this ministry was to establish and carry through a national strategy for innovation, for the application of research and development (R & D) in key sectors to overcome Britain's legacy of technological backwardness.[10] This grandiose objective, which was to some extent in conflict with the precise and limited sponsorship functions also assigned to the department, was never achieved. After a troubled early period, the ministry began to take over sponsorship functions for an increasingly wide range of industries from the Board of Trade, until it emerged later in the decade as a Department of Industry, with prime sponsorship responsibility for virtually the whole range of manufacturing industry. The transfer of this function from the traditionally *laissez-faire* Board of Trade to the newer and much more interventionist ministry was to have considerable repercussions on government-industry relations—but this is to anticipate.

However, the main point about structural intervention is that, even if government gets it right, the results take an enormously long time to show themselves. To generate a new breed of managers is the task of a decade, at least. To achieve a faster diffusion of new techniques, of the results of R & D, to carry through to fruition a major rationalisation in a single industrial sector—these are tasks with a five-year rather than a single-year horizon. So at best the efforts of the DEA, Neddy and others in the industrial area could be expected to give Britain a better industrial base for the 1970s. They could not be expected to make a major contribution to solving the economic crisis of the mid-1960s.

Moreover, as a decision taker in the commercial sphere, or as an effective partner with industry, government had—and still has—some major limitations. Commerce is all about risk taking. If you are right 51% of the time, the mistakes you make in the other 49% will be forgiven you. The political world is not like that. The ultimate sin in a civil servant's calendar is putting his minister in a situation where he cannot convincingly answer a hostile parliamentary question. Thus, especially in an area with which he is unfamiliar, a civil servant is predisposed to caution. The process of decision making is in any event much slower in government than in business, since government operates typically through a whole series of committees representing divergent departmental interests, culminating in the Cabinet. In business, in contrast to government, responsibility for decisions is normally delegated to individuals, committees playing an advisory role. Thus, all too often, governments prove too slow at taking commercial decisions, through searching too long for certainty in a situation some of the elements of which can never be known.

But, paradoxically, while governments are slow to take decisions, their sights are normally set on a much shorter time-scale than those in business. The career-span of a minister is a short one. It is unusual to remain in the same post for more than, say, two-and-a-half years (the average is about half this). During that time one's reputation is likely to be made or irretrievably lost—and performance in Parliament, where a minister is constantly on trial, is crucial. So it is a rare minister who is going to concentrate on long-term planning decisions to the detriment of short-term perceived performance. Civil servants of course have a longer time-span of responsibility. But civil servants exist to serve ministers. Thus, inevitably, the main concentration of effort and resources in any government department is likely to be in the solution of immediate short-term problems.

All of this may help to explain why Labour's insistence on a more interventionist role for government in the business arena—so-called 'positive government'—produced disappointing results in the mid-sixties. The policy was not basically misconceived. But there were unrealistic expectations about the speed at which changes could be made, an underestimation of the changes needed in government itself, and above all a failure to appreciate the interconnection between macro and micro policies.

THE REGIONAL DIMENSION

Before developing this point, which is crucial to any understanding of this period, it is worth saying a little bit about regional planning, for here again fundamental attitudes in government effectively frustrated what was intended to be a major exercise in structural change and devolution in decision taking. During the late 1950s and early 1960s there had been much discussion of the diversity of economic conditions between the different parts of the UK. In south-eastern England and the midlands the normal economic problem was overemployment, congestion and inflation. In northern England, Scotland, Wales and Northern Ireland the typical situation was one of a decaying industrial structure, under-employment and emigration. This fundamental imbalance—the other regions falling somewhere in between these two extremes—rendered the overall management of demand very difficult. A policy designed to reduce inflation in London and Birmingham was liable to produce a slump in Glasgow and Newcastle. What was needed, therefore, was some form of regionally differentiated economic policies, stronger than the measures which had been operated for a long time by the Board of Trade, to steer new investment away from the boom areas towards the depressed regions.

A second point which had become very clear was that the problems of underdevelopment were complex and embraced a number of factors. New investment was not likely to take place on a sufficient scale in the depressed regions, even with generous tax incentives, unless measures were taken to improve the infrastructure: housing, education and hospital facilities, transport, town planning and amenities like new shopping centres—all these had a major role to play in the regeneration of Britain's run-down regions.

Thus the intention of the new regional planning structure described above (which had indeed in part been foreshadowed by the previous Tory administration) was to enable integrated regional development plans to be produced which could be slotted into and reconciled with an overall national plan; these plans would enable the regeneration of those regions most in need of it, a transfer of jobs and resources between regions, and a certain degree of devolution in decision making about land-use planning.

As we shall see, the role of regional planning in the 1965 National Plan was in the event comparatively minor, though each region was in time to produce its own development plan. Given the shortage of time available this was not surprising. What was more disappointing was the failure of regional planning to survive the demise of the National Plan (see below) or to play any significant role in any future planning exercise. Though the regional planning councils and boards survive, their role has been marginal. Why has this been?

One factor certainly was the absence of any links at any time between Neddy and the regional councils. The NEDC and NEDO have never concerned themselves with the regional dimension of planning. But of more significance, almost certainly, has been the attitude of Whitehall. It was always clear that the regional planning boards, made up of civil servants with full-time executive roles, would be much more important than the councils, consisting of part-time non-elected local worthies. The idea was that the different departments would establish strong horizontal links at regional level, so that decisions affecting, for example, transport and housing policy would be taken in an integrated way. In fact, however, in every case the traditional vertical links within departments proved too strong. A departmental civil servant would refer upwards to his ministry headquarters in London rather than to his regional colleagues in other departments. The centralist tradition in the British civil service proved too strong for Labour's original vision of a complex of 'bottom-up' English regional plans (in Scotland, Wales and—in very different circumstances—Northern Ireland, the situation has been a bit different).

Of course, even if regional planning had developed as originally intended, the time horizons for any major change for the better in the nation's economic structure would have been at least as long as in the industrial area. So one comes back again to the question of short-term ways of solving the structural imbalance posed above.

DEVALUATION OR DEFLATION?

Two solutions are left—devaluation or deflation. By deflating demand one reduces imports, and gives a stimulus to exports, but at the cost of employment and—in the long run most important of all—investment. Deflation had been the traditional way of solving balance-of-payments crises up to 1960, and it had contributed to Britain's chronic problem of underinvestment (and therefore low productivity) and low growth, thus increasing the liability to future crises. In the conventional wisdom of the mid-1960s, it was a cure worse than the disease. And the problem was that even the comparatively mild (and, as it turned out, inadequate) attempts to damp down overheating in the economy during 1965—largely through increasing interest rates and imposing certain fiscal constraints—tended to depress investment rather than consumption.

The remaining solution was devaluation, either by fixing a new lower rate for sterling on the foreign exchanges, or letting it find its own level by 'floating'. A successful devaluation would, at a stroke, stimulate the necessary transfer of resources by making exports cheaper and/or more profitable, and imports dearer. On the other hand, at a time of overheating it would risk giving a further twist to the inflationary spiral by adding to the cost of living so far as imported goods were concerned.

By 1965 most expert opinion had come to the conclusion that, as the pound was manifestly overvalued, devaluation was sooner or later inevitable; clearly the growing army of speculators believed so. Moreover, the potential benefits of devaluation on the balance of payments outweighed the inflationary risks, though it would be better if devaluation took place when there was some slack in the economy.

So far as is known, the first time since 1949 when ministers seriously considered devaluation as an option was immediately after the Labour election victory of October 1964.[11] But when the decision was taken not to devalue, on political rather than economic grounds (the Prime Minister was concerned, among other things, about the effect on the USA, with whom we were negotiating a loan), all discussion of the subject within the government machine was banned.

What is not so well known is that at the very first meeting of the NEDC Selwyn Lloyd had also indicated that this was one topic which would not be allowed onto the Council's agenda. The reason for the caution shown by both governments is clear. If it was known that devaluation was an option under consideration the speculators would move into action, thus possibly forcing the government's hand before it had completed its evaluation. Nevertheless, the prohibition had serious effects. It meant that Whitehall had no contingency plans available for when the 'unmentionable' (referred to by that name increasingly frequently in Whitehall at that time) happened.

Such was the background against which George Brown's National Plan was prepared during 1965—a steadily worsening macro-economic situation to which the government had no answer, since it rejected the available options; while the micro policies on which it was concentrating were for the most part geared to a much longer time-scale. The first drafts of the Plan showed clearly that the government had a strategic choice: the price of continued growth would be a devaluation. This was not a message which was to appear in the Plan's published version.

THE NATIONAL PLAN...

At the time when the Plan was nearing completion, in the summer of 1965, the government was enjoying what proved to be a short-lived and fortuitous respite from its troubles. Pressure on the pound lifted, and at the same time the public opinion polls started to move in Labour's favour. For the first time since the end of 1964 it began to look as if Labour could get an enhanced majority in a general election. The temptation to use the Plan as a kind of election manifesto, a glossy brochure for 'Great Britain Ltd' rather than a basis for hard decision taking, proved irresistible. In the editing for presentation to the NEDC and eventual publication, the hard edges were rounded off, the awkward questions glossed over, and much of the potential value of the Plan for policy making both at national level and by enterprises thereby lost. Though the Plan undoubtedly did help the government to win a substantial majority in the 1966 election, that was a poor exchange, even from Labour's point of view, for the real value that it could have had.

That said, the National Plan[12] in its published version, which came out in September 1965, was by no means a worthless document. It covered a wider span than the Green and Orange Books, since it included chapters on different aspects of public expenditure, a detailed assessment of the prospects facing different industries, and a check-list of actions required by government and industry if the Plan objectives were to be met. The Plan also embraced regional planning objectives and prices and incomes policy.

The method was to choose a growth target—a 25% increase in national output by 1970, or 3.8% per annum (slightly more modest than the Green Book target)—and check it for feasibility with industry via the EDCs and other bodies. The work on the Plan revealed that the sum total of industries' own growth expectations (unlike the NEDC Plan, the industrial inquiry for the National Plan covered virtually the whole of industry) came to less than 25% by 1970. But in the course of dialogues between the industries and government planners the industrial figures were edged up to conform with the central forecast. How far this represented a genuine conversion of industry to higher growth remains open to doubt.

To meet the growth target, productivity would need to grow by 3.4% per annum, but industries' own projections of the likely growth remained at the NEDC forecast of 3.2%. This meant that 800,000 more workers would be required over the period, while the maximum likely to be available would be 400,000. Half this gap could be bridged by tapping unused reserves of manpower in the less prosperous regions. But it was clear that manpower would be a problem. Also, ominously, though little commented on at the time, practically the whole net additional demand for manpower was expected to come from public administration and the public service sector, such as health and education.

To promote the mobility which would be needed in the tight labour situation foreseen, the government proposed to step up investment in training, and to bring in wage-related unemployment benefits to complement its measures for redundancy compensation; such measures, it was thought, would soften trade union opposition to necessary redundancies, and thus aid mobility. It was clear that there would be heavy demand for additional skilled labour to meet the Plan targets. There would need to be an expansion of the Industrial Training Boards established in the 1964 Industrial Training Act.[13]

Among measures needed to raise industrial efficiency, special emphasis was given to the scope for import saving schemes, standardisation, export promotion (the government had recently set up a British National Export Council to help here), quicker movement of exports, rationalisation, public purchasing, better industrial management, and the application of science and technology. There was also much emphasis on the better use of labour generally, and oblique references to the need to tackle overmanning and restrictive labour practices in some industries. A 'norm' for wage and salary increases of 3-3½% a year was postulated. The Plan made no allowance for price inflation.

A good deal of attention was inevitably given to the balance of payments. A deficit of around £400 million anticipated for 1965 would need to be replaced by a surplus of £200-250 million by 1970, with debts of £900 million falling due for repayment between 1967 and 1970. This required the stabilisation of the growth of imports at the 1960-4 average of 4% per annum, despite the much faster growth foreseen for output. Exports would need to grow by 5¼% per annum, compared with 4% forecast on existing policies. Investment would naturally need to grow a lot faster than gross national product, and personal consumption substantially less—by 3.2% in fact.

The broad outlines of the Plan were not dissimilar from those of the NEDC Green Book, but it covered a much broader canvas and went into much more detail, while the check-list of action required was a good deal more specific than anything in the NEDC Orange Book. But it suffered from some fatal ambiguities. A spurious consistency was achieved in the industrial inquiry, which did not do justice to the many interesting and important deviations which emerged from the dialogue between government and industry. The Plan purported to present a very clear picture of the terminal year, 1970, but gave no indication of the path to be followed in the intervening period—in sharp contrast to the plans normally drawn up in business, where greater emphasis is given to the early years and where less precision is expected in the longer term. As with the NEDC Plan, the weakest section was that dealing with the balance of payments. There was no credible explanation of how the growth rate for exports was to be lifted from 4% to 5¼% a year (assuming no change in the exchange rate!).

A similar ambiguity surrounds the central 25% figure, variously described as a target or a forecast. It was clearly not widely accepted in industry as a credible forecast, and even within government decisions were seen to be being taken by departments which were not in line with the Plan, so that it was clearly not perceived as a control document for Whitehall. Perhaps the only sector of the economy which took the Plan seriously were the nationalised industries, who tended to base their investment plans on it. As a result, the nation was to experience a major glut of electrical supply capacity in the late 1960s, leading to an inevitable cutback in the early 1970s—precisely the kind of 'boom-and-bust' sequence which planning was supposed to eliminate.

...AND ITS AFTERMATH

Thus, by and large, the National Plan was a wasted exercise. This was a great pity. After the major investment in time, energy and expertise which had gone into it, improvements could certainly have been made during the regular review process which was foreseen in the Plan. But unfortunately this was not to be. The six months following the Plan's publication were a period of static output and productivity. During the summer of 1966 renewed pressure on the pound developed, and partly due to inattention by ministers in the euphoria and exhaustion following the election victory in March, things were allowed to deteriorate to the point in July when the economy faced a massive crisis of confidence.

In this crisis, the Cabinet was divided. George Brown and a small group of ministers argued for devaluation as the only alternative to deflation. They were over-ruled, largely due to the insistence of the Prime Minister and the Chancellor. Instead, a massive series of deflationary measures was announced, including heavy cuts in public investment, tighter building controls, increased taxes on consumption, and higher bank rate. What was left of the private investment boom was killed overnight. The National Plan was plainly in ruins, and was publicly renounced by its architect George Brown, who then changed places with the Foreign Secretary, Mr Michael Stewart.

The economy went into its most severe 'stop' phase since the war. The ambitions for faster growth kindled and fanned by both the major political parties since 1960 withered. And just over a year later, in the midst of yet another sterling crisis, the Chancellor, Mr Callaghan, announced that the pound would have to be devalued by 14.3%, and then left the Treasury to take over the Home Office. The sacrifice of growth for sterling had been in vain.

## NOTES

1 Northern, North-West, Yorkshire & Humberside, East Midlands, West Midlands, South-West, East Anglia, South-East. In Scotland and Wales the council chairmen were the relevant Secretaries of State. In Northern Ireland the structure was somewhat different again.
2 Though the councils and boards have shown a certain survival quality. Though completely bypassed in the reform of local government in the early 1970s, and though the regional development plans prepared for the DEA were largely ignored, they remain in existence—the only important DEA-created structure to do so. The chairmanship of the boards, incidentally, after the demise of the DEA, passed to the Department of the Environment.
3 EFTA was created after the failure of the negotiations to create a European free trade area in the late 1950s. It was a 'mini' free trade area embracing the UK, the Scandinavian countries, Switzerland, Austria and Portugal.
4 This tendency was of course reinforced by the structural weaknesses in the economy due to underinvestment, which meant that in boom conditions we ran up against capacity shortages and inability to supply goods—particularly high-technology capital equipment.
5 Speculation was not only the work of foreign bankers and exchange dealers—the so-called 'gnomes of Zurich'. A large part of it consisted of commercial firms—British and overseas—timing the payment of bills for goods or services according to whether they thought the value of a currency on world exchanges was about to go up or down, as a matter of normal commercial prudence. This is the so-called 'leads and lags' effect.
6 The signatories on the employers' side were the British Employers Confederation, the Federation of British Industries, the National Association of British Manufacturers, and the Association of British Chambers of Commerce. During the following year the first three of these merged to form the Confederation of British Industry (CBI).
7 When I went into industry after leaving the DEA in 1967, I was surprised to find a quite common belief that prices could only be increased if the NBPI explicitly sanctioned it. I am not aware if NBPI officials did anything to disabuse industrialists of this illusion, which flatteringly exaggerated the institution's power.
8 This was the General's second veto. An earlier attempt to enter the Community made by Mr Macmillan had encountered the same fate. (The still earlier effort to establish a European free trade area embracing the EEC had similarly been vetoed by the French.)
9 The main tax changes brought in by the Labour Government were the introduction of

Capital Gains Tax, Corporation Tax and the Selective Employment Tax (SET). Although these taxes had a considerable influence on the overall business climate, none of them is directly relevant to the theme of this book. Incidentally, none of them was discussed in the NEDC prior to introduction—though there was discussion of a fourth innovation, the Regional Employment Premium. SET was abolished by the 1970-4 Conservative Government and replaced by Value Added Tax (VAT).

10 For a fuller analysis of government policy on innovation and technology during this period, see my *The Innovators* (Penguin, Harmondsworth, 1967).

11 As opposed to 'floating' which was considered in the early 1950s—the so-called 'Robot Plan'—but rejected by the then Conservative Government.

12 For a fuller analysis, see Appendix 4.

13 In the event, the 'manpower gap' turned out to be a good deal wider, due to the reduction in working hours and increases in holidays negotiated at this time by a number of trade unions. In the past, reductions in the basic working week had tended to lead to increased overtime rather than a reduction in actual hours worked, and both the Green Book and the National Plan had implicitly assumed this would continue to be the case. But in fact for the first time a significant number of British workers decided to opt for increased leisure in place of increased pay. This imposed an extra constraint on growth unforeseen by the planners.

# 3 1966-1972: Planning in the Doldrums

The period between the abandonment of the National Plan in July 1966 and the abandonment of the $2.80 exchange rate for sterling in November 1967 was a bleak one for both country and government. The economy entered its severest postwar recession. The government floundered in a welter of unpopularity without any visible strategy. The obsequies on the National Plan were bitter and derisive, and for the first time since the 1950s 'planning' once again became a dirty word in the political vocabulary. The failure of the economy to conform in any apparent way to any of the Plan's predictions was commented on extensively by political and economic commentators, but there was little serious analysis of what had actually gone wrong.[1]

Among those concerned with the implementation of economic strategy and planning there were considerable changes of cast. Most importantly, Michael Stewart replaced George Brown as First Secretary of State in charge of the DEA and chairman of the NEDC. He brought with him a very different style—more methodical, more orderly, less adventurous, less boisterous, less creative. Under him the DEA settled down within the Whitehall machine as primarily a co-ordinating rather than a 'doing' or innovative department, with overall responsibility for prices and incomes policy, the approach to Europe, industrial policy co-ordination and regional development. Incomes policy acquired an added importance in the new economic climate. The crisis 'package' of July 1966 not only established the 'early warning' system of income and price notification referred to in the previous chapter, but also introduced a six-month wage and price freeze followed by a further six months of 'severe restraint', backed up by legislative sanctions.

These measures gave increased importance to the NBPI, for one of the main loopholes in the structure of wage control being erected was via so-called 'productivity bargaining', in which wage increases were paid in return for demonstrable increases in productivity through, for example, the 'buying-out' of traditional restrictive practices. The NBPI issued an important report in December 1966 which established the criteria which would enable a productivity bargain to receive governmental approval during the period of restraint.

Sir Robert Shone, the first director-general of the NEDO, had resigned in mid-1966, and had been replaced by a less reflective, more ebullient character, Mr (now Sir) Frederick Catherwood. Catherwood, unlike Shone, was no economist but an industrialist. Managing director of British Aluminium, he had been brought into government by George Brown as chief industrial adviser at the DEA. When he left the DEA his functions there were divided between Mr (now Sir) Ronald McIntosh, deputy secretary in charge of industrial policy, and myself, in charge of the team of industrial advisers.[2]

The planning vacuum left by the collapse of the National Plan had a number of institutional implications. To a marked degree, power tended to flow back from Whitehall to Neddy. During 1965 the main employer organisations had merged to create a single all-industry organisation called the Confederation of British Industry (CBI), designed to match the TUC in authority and influence. This strengthening of the employers' voice *vis-à-vis* Whitehall had an immediate influence on the tone of discussion at the NEDC, where the CBI spokesmen were not slow to voice their dissatisfaction at the way things were going. After the failure of the National Plan ministers became defensive at the Council. Almost the only significant economic measure brought in during the year was the Regional Employment Premium, which subsidised jobs in the development areas.

If discussions at the Council tended to be arid and unproductive during this period, in the EDCs things tended to go rather better, though they too were affected by the planning blight. But the vacuum of thinking at the macro level led to increased interest at the micro level in promoting industrial efficiency. Some EDCs sought to act rather as productivity consultants, and there was a rash of EDC-sponsored publications on various aspects of business efficiency (a booklet on stock control produced by the Distributive Trades EDC, entitled *Gold In Your Hands*, proved a best-seller).

It was also a great time for political gimmickry. The Prime Minister personally sponsored and chaired two National Productivity Conferences at Lancaster House in London, attended by some seventy delegates selected on a kind of 'expanded NEDC' basis, with the NEDO acting as the secretariat. After the first meeting Mr Wilson described the Conference as 'a kind of industrial parliament' and implied it would be a continuing institution, but after the second meeting he appeared to lose interest and nothing more was heard of it.

DEVALUATION AND ITS EFFECTS

The crisis which brought about sterling's devaluation and the end of James Callaghan's chancellorship was started by the Six Days' War between Israel and the Arab states. But if it had not been that, it would have been something else.[3] Sterling's health had become so delicate that the least disturbance to world trading patterns was likely to send it into a relapse. (In July 1966 it had been a strike of seamen in support of a wage claim; in July 1965 a single month's bad trade figures.) In the event, the 1967 devaluation was to give the UK a five-year reprieve from balance-of-payments crises, though this was hardly apparent at the time. (In fact, it was not until June 1969 that the balance of payments finally turned round, but thereafter the improvement was dramatic by any standards.)[4]

By accident, Britain had chosen a good time to devalue, when there was enough slack in the economy to hold back the inflationary pressures due to higher import costs and to take advantage of the new opportunities opened up in export markets. The new parity rate, $2.40, was a reasonably competitive one. The new Chancellor, Mr Roy Jenkins, formerly Home Secretary (he changed posts with Mr Callaghan, just as a year before Michael Stewart had changed posts with George Brown), had been one of the ministers arguing in favour of devaluation in the crucial Cabinet meeting of July 1966. His strategy during the two and a half years of his chancellorship—until Labour's election defeat in June 1970—was clear and unambiguous: to use the balance-of-payments opportunity created by devaluation to build up a surplus and pay off the debts accumulated by his predecessor. This necessitated holding down domestic consumption and allowing the recovery in investment and jobs to come through exports rather than internal demand. It was an austere policy, setting little store by initiatives at the micro level. While undoubtedly successful in its objectives—by the end of the decade Britain had begun to repay the debts incurred in earlier years, and was running a payments surplus substantially greater than foreseen in the National Plan—it is arguable that the internal austerity required cost Labour the 1970 election, as well as the investment needed to provide sustained long-term growth.

Exports grew rapidly in 1968, pulling the whole economy up with them, but less fast thereafter as the effects of devaluation wore off. The export recovery did not however lead to an investment boom, and industrial production virtually stood still in 1969 and 1970, which on postwar trade-cycle form should have been boom years like 1954/5, 1959/60 and 1964/5.

A further alarming aspect of this period was the first sign of the wage explosion which was to gather force in the 1970s. After the six-month freeze in the second half of 1966, the six-month period of 'severe restraint' had been characterised by a 'nil norm'—that is to say, the only increases permitted were those which met certain criteria such as those contained in the NBPI's 'productivity bargaining' guidelines. These expedients proved relatively successful, though unpopular. But the government lacked the determination to maintain the policy, and in mid-1967 reverted to the system of 'early warning', with the power to delay settlements for up to seven months on NBPI advice, but with no powers actually to prevent or limit increases as opposed to delaying them.[5] In the subsequent period prices and incomes policy tended to wither away, and the NBPI began to lose influence, until it was abolished by the incoming Conservative Government after June 1970.

In retrospect the readiness to abandon prices and incomes policy must be seen as one of Labour's major mistakes in this period. During 1968 and 1969 the rise in wages was not unreasonable, given the higher costs brought about by devaluation. But impatience was growing at the slow rise in British living standards and the relatively low level of economic activity, and towards the end of 1969 this impatience found expression in an eruption of wage demands for exceptionally large amounts. (The wage explosion was part of a worldwide trend, which Britain would in any case have found difficulty in avoiding.) In a pre-election situation the government was in no mood for trouble on the wages front, especially as it had no pre-election boom to boast of, such as the Tories had had in 1955, 1959 and 1964. (The Chancellor had in any case announced in his 1969 Budget speech that the power to delay wage awards was being dropped.) As a result, settlements in the late winter of 1969-70 averaged 12%—a foretaste of worse to come.

The other main feature of Roy Jenkins's chancellorship was a series of measures designed to ease overseas constraints on Britain's balance of payments. Defence commitments outside Europe were reduced very substantially, and in the 1968 Basle agreement the long-standing problem of the 'sterling balances'—the credits held with the Bank of England by sterling area governments which were normally immediately cashable, and thus posed a threat to sterling at moments of crisis—was eased by the provision of standby credits from the Bank of International Settlements. In effect the Basle agreement signalled the end of sterling's historic role as a reserve currency—a role Britain's economy was no longer strong enough to support.[6]

The role of the DEA and of NEDC in economic policy during the Jenkins era was comparatively marginal. The DEA was in any case in decline. In August 1968 Michael Stewart returned to the Foreign Office and was replaced at the DEA by Mr Peter Shore, at that time a relatively unknown and inexperienced politician. The Prime Minister took over the chairmanship of the NEDC himself, and Roy Jenkins became a member—though there is no evidence that he regarded this as a very important part of his responsibilities. The hostility of the Treasury towards the now seriously weakened DEA (which was shortly to lose responsibility for prices and incomes policy to the newly strengthened Department of Employment under Mrs Barbara Castle) remained.

Friction soon developed within the Council between the CBI and Mr Shore and his fellow-minister Mr Anthony Wedgwood Benn, Minister of Technology, over their proposed Industrial Expansion Act, which would give the government the powers and money to set up big joint ventures with companies of their choosing. This Act represented a major step towards selective intervention in the private sector, going a long way beyond the IRC or anything envisaged in the National Plan. The CBI felt that Fred Catherwood was departing from the objectivity required of his office by appearing to support this controversial measure. (The Act, although brought in by the Labour Government during 1968, was in fact little used during the remaining lifetime of the government.)[7]

More serious frictions were to develop during 1969 between the government and the TUC, over Barbara Castle's abortive proposals for trade union legislation. This episode, following the report of the Donovan Commission on trade unions and employers associations in mid-1968, caused the biggest internal split within the Labour Party since 1960, and soured relations between the party and the TUC into the 1970s, with fateful consequences for the party's political stance in the first half of the next decade, as we shall see.[8] In the end the Prime Minister had to abandon the proposed legislation. Ironically, the decision to abandon the last vestiges of prices and incomes control in 1969 was taken in order to clear the decks for legislation on trade unions, so that with the abandonment of the legislation the government lost out on both fronts.

All these major traumas were taking place offstage, so far as Neddy was concerned, during the last two years of the Labour administration. There was conflict within the government between those who wanted more detailed intervention in industry—Messrs Benn and Shore, fitfully supported by the Prime Minister—and the opposition led by the Chancellor; and between those who wanted to bring Britain's system of industrial relations under some kind of legal constraint—the Prime Minister, Mrs Castle, up to a late hour the Chancellor—and those who feared the political consequences—notably Mr Callaghan. Racked by internal dissension, the government was drifting nearer and nearer to the next election. At the end of 1969 there was a last-minute closing of ranks (or rather, papering-over of differences), and Mr Wilson went to the country in June 1970, fortified by what proved to be totally misleading public opinion polls, to go down to unexpected defeat.

'THE TASK AHEAD'

During this period of confusion, disarray and economic disappointment (except on the balance of payments), there was one significant planning initiative. Early in 1969, after several months' discussion in the NEDC, and considerable prompting from CBI and TUC—both of whom, for different reasons, wanted an opportunity to probe and influence government policy—the DEA published *The Task Ahead: An Economic Assessment to 1972*.[9]

Before describing and analysing this document, it is worth saying a little about the background. After the demise of the National Plan, there was a good deal of discussion behind the scenes in Whitehall and elsewhere among the experts about the desirability of producing a new kind of planning document. Many of us (I was party to some of these discussions) felt that after the *hubris* and arrogance of the National Plan had been punctured, and expectations were low, it would be a propitious moment to start working on a non-political, realistic plan; especially after the main constraint to growth, the necessity of maintaining an unrealistic parity for sterling, had gone.

One reason for this belief was that during the mid-1960s, while national planning was going through its traumas, the vogue for corporate planning—with techniques largely imported from the USA—was sweeping British (and indeed European) industry. A Society for Long-range Planning, established with DEA support in 1965, had enrolled a large number of corporate planners in the business area, and was going from strength to strength. Corporate planning and financial control were the two fastest growing disciplines in the growing number of business schools. It seemed to me and others that the state should try to learn from the successful planning ventures of the business sector, and that a credible national forecast would help the corporate planners in making their market projections. There should thus be the basis of a fruitful exchange of ideas.

There was considerable hesitation in government circles. This was a peculiarly difficult moment to forecast, we were told. Until the French veto settled the matter at the end of 1967, there was a major and legitimate doubt about one vital assumption—would Britain be a member of the EEC or not, and if so on what terms? Above all, there was the problem of the growth target. A realistic figure would be so low as to be a political embarrassment, especially after the National Plan and Green Book figures; but a high figure would carry no political credibility. Should we not wait until the economy looked better before venturing on such troubled waters again?

As against this, however, it could be argued that the purpose of planning was not to win political points, but to identify future problems so that they could be tackled in advance. That, after all, is why businesses plan (though business plans have the great advantage that they do not have to be published, so that failures in forecasting are an embarrassment only internally). Second, why should it be assumed that the end-product of a plan should be a faster growth rate? Many other objectives could be assigned to a national plan: better allocation of national resources, improved productivity, strengthening the balance of payments, identifying and removing obstacles to efficiency, enabling the business sector—public and private—to forecast better, by trying to remove one major element of uncertainty in their planning environment, and so on. Britain needed all of these, whatever the growth rate of the economy. A well-constructed plan should be able to help, not least in easing the 'stop-go' blight on private investment.

It was also necessary to help government take the right decisions in formulating its own public expenditure programmes. As we have seen, since the beginning of the 1960s the UK had been operating a five-year rolling programme for public expenditure. This exercise had pre-dated, and outlived, the Green Book and the National Plan. Conducted in conditions of some secrecy by the Treasury—as mentioned above, the attempt to transfer the responsibility for public investment to the DEA failed—it had never really been integrated with these exercises. The NEDC, for example, almost never discusses public expenditure programmes. But clearly, the more the government could find out about the forecasts and plans of the business sector, the more likely it was to be able to reach the right decisions on its own investment programmes.

There would thus seem to be a strong case for a dialogue between planners in government and in the major corporations, and for government to publish where possible its own forecasts of the development 'of the national economy, as an aid to the corporate planners; the exchange of information and ideas should be two-way, but it was up to government to establish the framework. Of course no framework could be a commitment—after the National Plan nobody would believe one anyway. It had to be recognised that if the economy diverged from the forecast path the government might have to take action; indeed, the more the government could reveal about its fall-back strategies in the event of divergence, the better. The lack of such strategies was one of the weaknesses of both the NEDC Plan and the National Plan.

For a new national plan to be useful, therefore, it had to be based on a wider range of consultation than in the first two plans. It had to distinguish clearly between targets and forecasts, and if targets were to be credible there must be some indication of the strategies which would enable the forecasts ('what will happen anyway') to be exceeded. The plan must be seen to carry authority within government if it was to have any credibility outside. Rather than pinning everything on a single growth projection, it would be more sensible to project alternative rates of growth. Ideally, if the price-tag in terms of policies for the different alternatives could be displayed, the plan would enable the nation to choose its economic future in a way hitherto denied it; for example, if higher growth could be demonstrated to depend on restraint in wages and short-term consumption, the interests represented around the NEDC table could in theory decide whether they thought the price worth paying. Moreover, the plan could and should address itself to other objectives beyond a faster rate of growth.

Finally, in conducting the dialogue with industry the national planners should seek to limit themselves to asking questions to which reasonably reliable answers could be given. The National Plan technique of presenting an identical questionnaire to all major firms and business sectors, whether the questions posed were relevant or not, had produced much information which was extremely dubious.

It also had to be recognised that different organisations planned to very different time-horizons. For light consumer goods or the distributive trades, for example, any plan which looked more than two or three years ahead had little relevance. Their world was too volatile. At the other extreme, basic industries like coal, steel or electricity needed to plan on a ten-year horizon or longer. The building of a new power station or steel mill could take five years or more. Thus the utility of a national plan which addressed itself only to a terminal period five years ahead, without any indication of what would happen in the intervening years, would be much less than that of a plan which—like most corporate plans—contained forecasts for a span of years.

Any new plan, therefore, had to be more modest, more flexible, more democratically constructed, than its two predecessors. It should take advantage of the fact that expectations were low and uncertainty about the future was great. And it should aim to be, not a one-off monument like the National Plan, but the starting-point for a continuing dialogue.

*The Task Ahead*, which was conceived by the DEA early in 1968, and published after lengthy discussions within the NEDC and elsewhere, went quite a long way along this road. It described itself as a 'planning document' rather than a 'plan'. The initial document set out government policies and the government's view as to the way the economy was going to develop. This was then discussed in some detail with a limited range of industries,[10] the industrial comment being combined with the economic assessment in a subsequent document, *Economic Prospects to 1972—A Revised Assessment* (in this book, both documents are considered together).

Thus the DEA's document was presented as a basis for discussion with industry, rather than a formal government commitment. The dialogue was extensive. There was a special meeting of the NEDC at Chequers to review the papers, a two-day meeting at Lancaster House with the EDC chairmen to review the relevant sector plans (an experiment which did not prove very successful), and a special conference at Henley between the DEA/NEDO planners and some selected corporate planners (I was by this time in charge of corporate planning at British Leyland and attended in that capacity).[11] The whole exercise was low-key, leisurely and reflective, especially by comparison with the hectic timetables enforced for the NEDC and National Plans.

*The Task Ahead* included the important innovation of making alternative projections—the so-called 'wedge'; a forecast of what would happen on unchanged policies, and an objective which if achieved would come nearer to meeting national aspirations. It focused on the constraints likely to be encountered in meeting the objective, and on what could be done to overcome them. The forecast chosen was for an average growth rate of $3\frac{1}{4}\%$ per annum (the so-called 'central case'), though there was some discussion of a possible worse outcome of under 3%, while the objective was set at 4%. In each case these were trend rates of growth. There was no attempt to predict the year-by-year path, or to build in assumptions about cyclical fluctuations.

The debate on growth rates may seem academic in retrospect, but it reflected major differences of opinion between the parties grouped around the NEDC table. Broadly speaking, from the inception of Neddy the TUC has argued for commitment to a high growth rate, with the proviso that government should be prepared to 'make it happen' by following *dirigiste* policies where necessary. (The TUC was indeed at this time arguing for a 6% growth rate, and only reluctantly accepted the lower figure.) The CBI, by contrast, has pleaded for a lower growth rate which will be credible, and which will not tempt government into interfering with the market economy more than absolutely necessary. Thus arguments on growth rates tend to reflect fundamentally different views on the nature of planning in a democracy—the extent to which it should be mandatory, normative or merely indicative. Given the background of mutual dissatisfaction in the Council at the time of discussions on *The Task Ahead*, for reasons analysed above, the growth rate proved a particularly intractable issue.

Among the major hurdles anticipated was, of course, the balance of payments. The objective was to move to a surplus of the order of £500 million a year while paying off some £2,000 million of accumulated debt. To help achieve this, the National Plan check-list of actions needed was approved and monitored. On the 'central case', it was assumed that imports would rise by 4% a year and exports by 5¾%. Half the projected 1972 payments surplus would come from the visible trade balance, the other half from invisibles and capital account.

Output per head was expected to rise by 2.9% per annum, against an actual 2.6% between 1961 and 1966. But the working population was not expected to grow at all during the plan period, in contrast to the 0.7% annual rise in the 1961-6 period. Consequently, on the 'central case' assumption, the nation's productive potential would grow by only 2.9% a year, though calculations were also made on the assumption that it might grow by as much as 3½% a year or as little as 2½%. (The margin between the forecast rate of growth and the increase in productive potential is of course made up by the bringing into use of unemployed workers and unused capacity.) As in the earlier plans, investment was forecast to grow substantially faster than national product, and personal consumption substantially less. The general profile of the economy, in short, differed little from that set out in the Green Book or National Plan, except that the growth figures were more modest.

The industrial estimates were derived from the 'central case' 3¼% per annum assumption, based on a continuation of past trends in output per man-hour and the improvements in exports and import-saving needed to support that rate. The estimates in the planning document were intended to be taken simply as a starting point for consultations with industry, which should lead to the exploration of the implications of different growth rate patterns. They were based on a complex process of disaggregation from the central forecast, using an input-output model of the economy to predict inter-industrial flows.

'ECONOMIC PROSPECTS TO 1972'

The dialogue with industry on the estimates took up most of 1969, and the result was *Economic Prospects to 1972—A Revised Assessment*, prepared by the government at the beginning of 1970. This document also took account of economic developments during 1969. This resulted in fairly marginal changes to the forecasts for GDP (central case), and the various constituent items in the balance of payments. (During 1969 the economy had moved into balance-of-payments surplus at last.) But the most important element in the industrial inquiry was the examination of capacity, and the attempt to identify possible bottlenecks as the economy expanded. This analysis was carried out much more thoroughly than ever before, and it revealed possible areas of difficulty in motors, chemicals and parts of engineering, the three key sectors from which increased exports were expected.

The dialogue with the motor industry, with which I was personally involved, was particularly interesting. The industry was trying to persuade government that if the domestic restrictions on hire purchase were lifted it would be able to achieve the economies of scale enjoyed by its Continental competitors. In order to examine this case, detailed exercises were carried out within the NEDO framework on the industry's effective capacity and productivity rates. Unfortunately I found that it was not possible to reconcile my company's corporate plan with the NEDO exercise, since the assumptions on market growth which we were asked to work on by the government were not those which I felt I could recommend as a realistic basis for forward planning to my company. This illustrates one of the dilemmas about the reconciliation of national and corporate plans. If government asks one to forecast what one's company will do on certain assumptions which one does not in fact believe are realistic, and which are not accepted as planning assumptions by one's company, of course one tries to answer the government's questions as honestly and conscientiously as one can (assuming one cannot persuade government to alter its assumptions); but, if the company itself is not using the same assumptions, it is unlikely to take the decisions needed to make the government's sums come right. And so it proved in this case.

This of course in no way invalidates the importance of the dialogue or the need to try to reach a consensus. But if there can be no genuine consensus, the worst thing is to try to conceal the fact—as happened in the Green Book and the National Plan—by following what is alleged to be the practice in Italian industry: producing one set of books for government and another for internal management of the enterprise. It is much better to have the dialogue in the open, and to record disagreements on assumptions openly—even if this seems to weaken the credibility of the government's planning. Otherwise, as happened with the National Plan, events will destroy its credibility much more savagely and irretrievably. And, of course, a 'low growth' consensus by industry can be self-fulfilling, even if based on faulty premisses; so it is right and proper, as the enthusiasts for planning were arguing in 1960, that government should have the opportunity of trying to influence their thinking in a more positive direction—which it can only do if it knows the thinking, and the reasons behind it.

In this second document assessments were made of the increase in resources which would flow from, and be required by, a modified 'central case' forecast of 3% per annum, and a 'higher case' target of 3¾%. To achieve the 3% rate, let alone the higher case, would require more investment than seemed likely to be forthcoming—and a restraint in domestic spending (by both government and consumers), which was about to be belied by the wage explosion and the expansion in the government's credit base and public consumption.

The planning document posed these and other problems fairly, and envisaged a detailed follow-up process of dialogue with industry. It seemed that at last planning had been set on a path of realism, and despite the initial difficulties (a lot of EDCs found difficulty in considering projections based on alternative assumptions, and tended to ignore the non-'central case' estimates), a convergence between national and corporate planning seemed at last under way.

But once again the planners were unlucky with their timing. In October 1969 the DEA was disbanded, medium and long-term planning reverting to the Treasury. This was an inconvenience, since *The Task Ahead* had been very much a joint DEA-NEDO initiative, and Treasury interest was minor. The 1970 Budget in no way reflected the discussions which had been going on at sector level on *Economic Prospects to 1972*. But much more important was the fact that the follow-up was overtaken by the June 1970 election, which produced a Conservative Government deeply antipathetic to any form of planning or interventionist policies. The follow-up, therefore, never took place in the form intended. Planning once again went into cold storage.

CONSERVATIVE GOVERNMENT AGAIN

The new government under Mr Edward Heath—he had succeeded Sir Alec Douglas-Home as leader of the Conservative Party before the 1966 election—was pledged to a policy of disengagement from industry in every way possible. The IRC was abolished; so was the NBPI. There were to be no more attempts at wage and/or price control. Many other quasi-governmental institutions went the same way. It seems a little strange in retrospect that Neddy did not follow them. (The other 'survivor' was the network of regional economic planning councils and boards.) In fact, although it was decided that NEDC should be kept in being as a convenient way of keeping the lines of communication open to the TUC and CBI, there was plainly no intention that Neddy should play an activist role, and NEDO officials were given no indication that their long-term future was assured. The new government did indeed institute an investigation into the EDCs, to see whether they should be maintained or not.

This investigation, which many friends of the little Neddies felt was, if anything, overdue, took place under the auspices of the NEDC co-ordinating committee which had been set up some time before, representing government, CBI, TUC and NEDO. The EDCs had grown from the

original nine to twenty-one, and not surprisingly their performances were
very uneven. Different people had expected different things from them.
Selwyn Lloyd had hoped that they would focus on specific issues like
restrictive labour practices, and that they would somehow shame the
unions into reform. In fact, in almost all the EDCs restrictive practices
remained a taboo subject.

George Brown, as we have seen, also hoped that they would act as
major agents for reform in their industries—hopes which were likewise
doomed to disappointment. Others saw the main role of the EDCs as
links in the national planning machinery—a role which some performed
well, others less so. Many of the industrialists, who tended to dominate
them, saw the EDCs as a means of lobbying government. The trade
unions, though unable in the main to make a major contribution to the
technical work of the little Neddies, nevertheless set great store by their
membership, which enabled them to discuss issues affecting their
members outside the normal collective bargaining context, and felt that
in this way they got closer to management than they could otherwise have
done. As for the sponsor departments, their attitude was ambivalent.
While on the one hand frequently irritated at the lobbying role adopted
by some of the EDCs, at the same time some of them found that as
members they could learn more about the details of their industries than
through the formal sponsoring channels in Whitehall.

Thus, for different reasons, most of the participants found the EDCs
useful bits of machinery. But how far could they be more than 'talking
shops'? During my time as the DEA official responsible for the little
Neddies, I was frequently asked the question: 'What have they actually
*done*? What *difference* have they made?' It was a question I found very
difficult to answer, and the investigators clearly found it no easier four
years later, in 1970. My private view was that about a third were doing a
very useful job, another third were marginally or potentially useful, and
a third should probably be wound up. I think I would have given the
same advice in 1970. But that was a subjective judgement I would have
been hard put to quantify.

Much depended on the ability of the chairman, and much on the
structure of the industry concerned. I served on two EDCs. One,
electrical engineering, was a rather oligopolistic industry with a strong
trade association. This had two consequences. It meant that, once we
have taken a decision or completed a report, the trade association
provided an effective mechanism for communication through the
industry. But it also meant that it was not easy for the EDC to establish a
role for itself apart from the trade association, on which it relied for
information and industrial contacts.

The other EDC, for the distributive trades, was at the opposite
extreme. There was literally no other organisation covering this sector.
Trade union organisation was weak, the sponsor department had no
strong links with the trades concerned, and there were something like 120
separate trade associations—most of them small, weak and understaffed.

We were thus filling a vacuum. This gave us great freedom in our discussions, and we were able to do quite a lot to promote the needs of the sector in Whitehall and to disseminate knowledge of business techniques. But we faced almost insuperable difficulties in communicating the results of our work throughout our huge, sprawling parish, and indeed probably the most important achievement of this EDC has been to act as the catalyst for the creation of a more effective trade association structure.

Thus, some EDCs operated in sectors which were neatly defined, but others did not. In all, but especially the latter group, there were problems in establishing a statistical basis on which performance evaluations—for example, the sector's achievement in exports and import substitution—could be assessed. Most of the EDCs' work was inevitably detailed and parochial; and, while they generated a great number of reports and recommendations, they had difficulty in communicating these to their constituents, and still greater difficulty in seeing that any action was taken on them. Government could reasonably complain—as ministers tended to do also from time to time on the NEDC—that while it was expected to act on Neddy recommendations, the other partners found it much easier to evade responsibility. This stricture applied at both macro and micro level.

Behind all this there was an undercurrent of thinking in Whitehall which was evident at the time of the National Plan, but was to grow more important in the early 1970s. This was to the effect that if planning was to go beyond the macro level, the planners had to have direct access to the decision makers. Decisions on business policy are not, and cannot be, made at sector level. They are made, and have to be made, at the level of the individual enterprise. Thus the proper concomitant to national planning should be a direct dialogue between government and large firms, on the French model. (The French also use sector planning—the so-called 'modernisation committees'—as well as direct government-to-firm quasi-contractual relationships.) Some very tentative steps were taken in this direction by the DEA and the Ministry of Technology during the mid-1960s—I recall participating in one such dialogue while at British Leyland—but they did not get very far. To those who thought in these terms, such as Mr Wedgwood Benn, the EDCs—however good—could have only a marginal role.

The investigation of the EDCs did not go into these broad philosophical questions, which in any case were quite out of tune with the thinking of the new government. It was much more a down-to-earth technical assessment of the contribution made by each individual EDC, on necessarily vague criteria. (How could one define the output of an EDC? On the number of papers emerging from it? On the number of recommendations accepted by government? On the quality of its forecasts?) In the event the little Neddies came out surprisingly well. Five were wound up (two more were to be started later by the Tory Government). The remaining sixteen were given a clean bill of health, but asked to report annually to the Council (surprisingly, this had not been required before). The basic structure was unchanged.

There is some evidence that the government was a little surprised, and maybe even a little impressed, by the attachment of both sides of industry to the EDCs, and indeed to the Neddy structure as a whole. Certainly the early astringency of the new administration towards the institution faded fairly soon, though the Council's role in policy making remained marginal—as indeed it had during Roy Jenkins's chancellorship. There was no great change in the climate at NEDC with the change in government; it merely became a few degrees colder.

THE CRISIS RETURNS

Tensions in any case were developing between the NEDC partners. Relations between the government and TUC rapidly became embittered when it became clear that the Cabinet was determined to push through an Industrial Relations Bill which was considerably stronger than that proposed by Barbara Castle, and subservently withdrawn by Harold Wilson. This Bill, which became law in 1972, was by far the most important element in policy-making in the early years of the Heath Government. It profoundly influenced, as we shall see, relations between the trade union movement and both major political parties, in a way that was to have fateful consequences for Britain's economic and political evolution in the early and mid-1970s. It was also to embitter relations between the TUC and the CBI, whom the unions justly or unjustly suspected of conniving with the Tories on this issue.

This partly explains the curmudgeonly response which the TUC gave to a potentially very important initiative undertaken by the CBI in July 1971. The CBI was under new leadership. The first director-general, Mr John Davies, had resigned to enter politics, and in the Conservative Government he was rapidly promoted from the back benches to head a new super-ministry formed by the merger of the Board of Trade and Ministry of Technology, the Department of Trade and Industry (DTI). John Davies was actively associated with the new Tory policy of disengagement from industry, the refusal to 'prop up lame ducks'—i.e. advance aid or assistance to industries or firms which through their own inefficiency were falling into bankruptcy.

His successor at the CBI was Mr (now Sir) Campbell Adamson, a steel industry man who had succeeded me as chief industrial adviser at the DEA in 1967, subsequently becoming deputy secretary in charge of industrial policy. He formed a close association with the CBI president, Sir John Partridge, chairman of Imperial Tobacco (subsequently Imperial Group). Together, they persuaded an overwhelming majority of the 200 largest CBI firms to accept a voluntary price standstill for twelve months to 31 July 1972, which in the event was to be extended to the end of October 1972. This action was taken with the approval of, but independently from, government.

The situation of the economy when the CBI initiative was launched was not good. The breathing space won by devaluation was beginning to be exhausted. The economy was stagnant, investment was languishing. Wage inflation had gathered pace since 1969, and was running at an annual rate of 12% with every sign of accelerating. For the first time, wage inflation and unemployment were seen to be rising simultaneously; whereas in the past deflation, whatever its unpleasing side-effects, had at least kept wages and prices down. Price inflation had reached 10%, but even so profits were sagging. The CBI's proposal to the Chancellor, Mr (now Lord) Barber, was that if the government would undertake a modest reflation of the economy, industry would hold prices level despite the wage pressure.

The Chancellor responded, and in a special mini-Budget timed to coincide with the CBI initiative he put back enough purchasing power into the economy to generate the beginnings of a recovery. But there was no response from the trade unions, and in the spring of 1972 the economy was rocked by a strike by the miners' union for higher pay, which resulted in a highly inflationary pay award of 21% from a special tribunal under Mr Justice Wilberforce.

By mid-1972 the economy was again in a desperate state. The renewed inflationary pressures had finally exhausted the gains won by devaluation, and the country once again faced a massive balance-of-payments problem, at a time when economic growth was still modest. The inflation was moreover eroding the profitability of major sectors of industry to a dangerous degree, the crisis stretching far beyond the expendable 'lame ducks' whose demise the government was prepared to see. The Conservatives' economic strategy had failed almost as dramatically as had Labour's in 1966. And, as in 1966, the bankruptcy of government brought Neddy back into the centre of the stage. Once again the wheel had gone full cycle.

NOTES

1 An honourable exception was Samuel Brittan's *Inquest on Planning* (PEP, London, 1967).
2 Sir Ronald is the current director-general of NEDO.
3 In fact a contributory factor was the advice of the European Commission, given during the negotiations for Britain's entry into the EEC, that sterling was overvalued. There was always a link between entry into the EEC and devaluation. The fact that France had eased her entry into the EEC on its establishment by devaluing the franc to strengthen her competitiveness was not lost on the 'European' lobby in British politics. Entry into the EEC was a crucial element in the economic strategy propounded by George Brown and the DEA. The idea that devaluation might be part of the 'entrance ticket' into the EEC gave it a respectability which it might not otherwise have had, and helped to soften resistance to the concept on the part of those—a majority in industry as well as in Parliament—who believed that Britain should join the European Community. Ironically, the French veto on the EEC negotiations was applied one week after the pound was devalued.
4 This was an example of what economists call the 'J-effect' of a devaluation on the balance of payments. The immediate effect of a devaluation, according to this theory, is negative. The *cost* of imports rises immediately, while it takes time to achieve the offsetting changes in the *volume* of exports and imports. However, unless the effects of the cheapening of the currency are completely offset by other factors such as internal inflation, experience suggests that in the long term the volume effects of a devaluation

more than outweigh the cost effects. And so it was on this occasion, though the wait was long and agonising.

5 The power to delay was extended in the 1968 Budget from seven months to twelve.

6 It has to be remembered that the late 1960s and early 1970s were a period of great turmoil on the international exchange front. A number of factors contributed. Prominent among them was the weakness of the US dollar, and the consequent strength of gold (until the Washington gold agreement of 1968 gold and dollars were freely interchangeable; in the Washington agreement the US government ended the free convertibility of dollars into gold, thus in effect ending the gold standard system in the form established at the 1944 Bretton Woods Conference.) The weakness of the dollar reflected in part the heavy costs of the Vietnam war, which the USA financed through printing money rather than raising taxation. This process, by which the world's liquid resources were greatly enhanced, contributed to the rising tide of world inflation. At the same time there was a steady move of money into the strong currencies, notably those of West Germany and Switzerland, which consequently had to be revalued upwards. The Basle agreement was thus a fairly minor aspect of a general realignment of the world's monetary structure which was taking place over this period, culminating in the so-called Smithsonian agreement in the autumn of 1971, which fixed new exchange rates between the major currencies. What necessitated the realignment was the weakness in relation to their commitments of the US dollar and sterling, and the growing strength of certain other currencies, notably the West German Deutschmark, the Swiss Franc and the Japanese yen.

7 With one possible exception—the use of the Act to bring into existence an aluminium-smelting industry in the UK, on the basis of government-subsidised cheap electricity.

8 For a brilliant account of the Labour Government's abortive attempt to bring in legislation on trade unions and industrial relations, see Peter Jenkins's *The Battle of Downing Street* (Charles Knight, London, 1970). The Donovan Commission, in its three-year study (it was appointed in April 1965) analysed in great depth the defects in the British industrial relations structure, and made a number of recommendations for reform; but the role assigned to government in the main report, unlike some of the minority reports, was fairly minor.

Barbara Castle saw a much more activist role for government in humanising and modernising Britain's industrial relations system, which she set out in a White Paper, *In Place of Strife—a Policy for Industrial Relations*, in January 1969. This contained suggestions for compulsory ballots before strikes could be called, for compulsory procedures to resolve inter-union disputes, and for a compulsory 'cooling-off' period before a strike was called, to allow conciliation to take place. Though the White Paper contained a number of other proposals, many of them favourable to the unions, it was these three which aroused the hostility of the TUC and of those Labour MPs (including some ministers) who were close to the unions. In the end, after a six-month agonising debate within the Labour movement which threatened to tear it apart, the Prime Minister was forced in June 1969 to withdraw the proposed legislation, in return for promises of self-reform by the TUC. During the subsequent and final twelve months of his administration—and during the early years of Opposition thereafter—Mr Wilson and his colleagues perforce gave a very high priority to mending their fences with the unions.

9 For a fuller analysis, see Appendix 5.

10 These were: mechanical engineering, machine tools, electrical engineering, paper and board, motor manufacturing, chemicals and electronics in the EDC sector; steel, energy, shipbuilding, aircraft, iron and steel castings in the sector not covered by EDCs; and invisible earnings.

11 The Henley conference recommended: a longer time-horizon; extended links between NEDO and individual planners, with regular exchange of views and forecasts leading, perhaps, eventually to a jointly serviced national econometric model; more recognition to be given in future national planning to changes in the international environment; increased coverage of changes in the EEC; forecasts of technological change; better manpower and investment studies in future national plans; preparation of a longer-term (ten-fifteen years) perspective, perhaps prepared with the assistance of a body outside government and NEDC; and, finally, improved communication of the results of national planning exercises to the business community.

# 4 1972-1976: Return to Planning

The situation facing the British Government in mid-1972 was as follows. The economy had started to pick up following the autumn Budget of the previous year, and despite the CBI price freeze industry's profits were also up. The first signs of an investment boom were beginning to appear. But the balance of payments was in bad shape. The pound sterling once again was evidently overvalued. Moreover, the country was facing rising import prices due to the worsening world inflation. In spite of the CBI action, prices were rising at a rate of 8½% a year, and there was no sign of any lessening in wage pressure. Indeed, after the surrender to the miners there was a grave danger of a stampede of other unions towards still higher wages; and the bitter climate created by the government's Industrial Relations Act seemed to preclude government-union co-operation. All the forecasts suggested that on present policies inflation would get worse.

The government faced some difficult choices. Moreover, time was short. The CBI's price restraint commitment was due to expire at the end of July, and a number of large firms were becoming extremely restive. Despite the general recovery of profits, some very large enterprises were in shaky financial condition. The government was under pressure to make use of the CBI's goodwill before it evaporated completely.

The first choice therefore was whether to continue the policy of expansion or not. Like Mr Maudling ten years before, Mr Barber decided to do so. He protected his sterling flank by deciding in June 1972 to let the pound float—in effect, a third postwar devaluation. (In the ensuing four years, the pound was to drop by a further 25% against the dollar.) Thus, with the sterling constraint finally removed, Britain began its second 'dash for growth' under a Conservative Chancellor. Taxes were cut, and—somewhat strangely for a Conservative Government—there were massive increases in public spending. The industrial production index, which had virtually stood still since 1969, rose by 3% in the second half of 1972 and by 7½% in 1973—the biggest rise in a decade.

The dash for growth required two major U-turns in economic policy to sustain it. First, the 'lame duck' policy of non-intervention in industry associated with John Davies had to be reversed by his successor at the

DTI, Mr Peter Walker, who returned to a policy of interventionism. The Conservatives' 1972 Industry Act reinforced and strengthened Labour's Industrial Expansion Act of 1968, which had caused so much controversy in the NEDC. These measures were forced by the collapse of Rolls-Royce and some other spectacular bankruptcies in the private sector. The state was having to pick up some of the major drop-outs from private enterprise in order to safeguard jobs and preserve the industrial structure.

The Act included provisions for special assistance to particular sectors or enterprises in regions of high unemployment, and aid for accelerated investment projects. Assistance could take the form of interest relief, or capital grants up to 20% of the cost of renewal of assets, for approved schemes. These discretionary grants were to be used—particularly under the next Labour Government—in a number of sectors where EDCs were active, notably in wool textiles (the pioneer project), ferrous foundries, clothing and machine tools. They provided a substantial fillip for the work of the little Neddies, which for the first time could back their persuasion of member-firms in their sectors with the promise of state cash.

PRICES AND INCOMES POLICY

The other major *volte face* was over prices and incomes policy. The Prime Minister convinced himself during the summer of 1972 that agreement had to be reached with the trade unions on a voluntary prices and incomes policy if inflation was to be held in check. He succeeded in imposing his views on a reluctant Cabinet—just as, eleven years before, an equally reluctant Tory Cabinet had accepted the U-turn on planning which led to the birth of Neddy.

Now, once again, Neddy was to be the instrument of change. During the summer and autumn of 1972 that body swung into frenzied action in an attempt to reach accord on a voluntary policy on wage and price restraint before the CBI initiative (extended for three months after the end of July) expired. Despite the continued ructions over the Industrial Relations Bill, which the unions were continuing to oppose vehemently— and, as it was to turn out, successfully—the TUC side at the NEDC agreed to co-operate in the search for a policy.[1]

Thinking in Britain at this time was much influenced by the experience of the USA. The administration of President Nixon, which had started life in 1968 with a policy of *laissez-faire*, non-intervention in business, and willingness to tolerate high levels of unemployment in order to reduce inflation, had itself made a spectacular U-turn in 1970, bringing in expansionist policies buttressed by measures to restrain wage rises and to limit profit margins. By 1972 these measures seemed to be having some success, and this fact had considerable influence with a Conservative Government about to undertake the same policy changes two years later than the Americans.

The work at Neddy was headed by a new director-general, Sir Frank Figgures, who had replaced Fred Catherwood the previous year. Sir Frank, a 'Treasury knight', was the first civil servant to hold this post. But in some ways he was an atypical one. In the mid-1960s, as general secretary of EFTA, he had shown considerable courage in resisting pressures from the British Labour Government to break the rules of that organisation.

Working parties were set up with representatives from government, TUC, CBI and NEDO to draw up outline policies for both pay and prices. In September the working parties reported to an NEDC steering group, consisting in effect of the Council less its independent members, chaired by the Prime Minister at 10 Downing Street. Mr Heath's handling of the operation was masterly. Not only did he begin to convince a suspicious TUC of the genuineness of his desire for a consensus; as the negotiations went on he seemed also to convince himself that the country could be run on a basis of mutual trust and co-operation between a Conservative Government and a strong but responsible trade union movement.

The negotiations were essentially between the Prime Minister and the TUC. The CBI, under a new and untried president (Mr Michael Clapham of ICI), made little contribution. Nor did the rest of the Cabinet contribute much. Of the senior ministers, probably only Peter Walker fully understood and shared his leader's new-found vision.

On wage ceilings, the TUC's thinking was not far removed from that of the government. But on prices there were difficulties. The TUC wanted a commitment to control—and if necessary subsidise—key food prices. But unfortunately, just at this time, grain prices were rising rapidly on world markets due to the spectacular failure of the Russian wheat harvest, with consequent heavy purchases by the USSR on world markets. The government was thus reluctant to give pledges which it would find hard to keep. (It has to be borne in mind that throughout the period of the Heath administration the terms of trade—the price of imports relative to that of exports—were moving against the UK, thus aggravating both the balance-of-payments and the inflation problems.)

Unfortunately between September and October the momentum of the exercise slackened. There was one good reason for this. During 1972 the UK had been making its third—and this time successful—bid to enter the EEC. The Prime Minister was personally deeply committed to this and heavily involved in the negotiations. He regarded it, with reason, as the great achievement of his administration.[2] During the autumn of 1972 Edward Heath and his government spent a great deal of time finalising the agreement to enter the European Community and on the necessary consequent measures, culminating in a major conference of the heads of government of the nine countries of the enlarged Community (Ireland and Denmark had joined with Britain) to chart the future course of Europe. Inevitably, but sadly, attention was diverted at a crucial time from the Neddy negotiations.

The government felt that time was against it, and that a prices and incomes policy had to be in place by the end of the year if the economy was to be put right. But at the October meeting of the steering group it was plain that agreement was still some way off. The TUC was insisting on a statutory policy for price control and a voluntary policy for income restraint. (It was also trying to get the government to abolish the Industrial Relations Act though this was almost certainly just a bargaining ploy.) At this point the Prime Minister lost patience, broke off the talks and announced a statutory policy for both pay and price restraint.

Opinions differ among the participants in these talks as to whether Heath's action was precipitate or not. Certainly the TUC seems to have been negotiating in good faith, and certainly there was a gulf of misunderstanding and mistrust on both sides which in the end proved fatal. But what is not clear is whether more time could have bridged the gap or not.

Opinions may also differ on whether in the event it mattered very much. For the policy unilaterally imposed by the government was in fact very close to what both sides had been negotiating about, and it was accepted without much demur by both CBI and TUC. The real failure in the talks was more subtle. The opportunity was missed to build a real understanding between Edward Heath and the unions which could have avoided the traumas which were to occur over pay policy at the end of 1973.

But this is to anticipate. The immediate aftermath of the breakdown of the talks at 10 Downing Street was deceptively calm, with a resigned acquiescence on all sides that the government had to do something, and that the measures proposed were reasonably fair. The structure established under the Counter-Inflation Acts of November 1972 and March 1973 owed much to the US model. There was a ninety-day standstill on prices, charges for services, pay, dividends and rents. This was known as Phase 1, and it proved (as have all the short-term 'freezes' imposed on pay and prices in postwar Britain) highly successful. This was despite the fact that prices of fresh food and imported raw materials remained uncontrolled, interest rates continued to fluctuate, and salary increments were unaffected by the freeze.

Phase 2, inaugurated the following March, established a pay-and-price code to be administered by two new statutory bodies, a Price Commission and a Pay Board. (Cynics said that the only reason why there were two bodies and not one was that the government did not want to seem to be resurrecting the NBPI, which it had summarily executed only two years previously. In fact the separation of the two functions meant that it was more difficult to establish an integrated strategy, and much more difficult to take into account the productivity questions which so preoccupied the Aubrey Jones Board.)

The main provisions of the code were that pay could not be increased by more than £1 a week plus 4% per annum, and that pay settlements could not take place more frequently than once a year; firms could recover in price rises not more than half any increase in labour costs; net profit margins from sales in the home market must not exceed their average level in the best two of the five preceding years; dividend rises were limited to 5% per annum. Fresh foods, imports, and exported goods and services were not subject to price control.

The main novelty in this operation was that for the first time government had at its disposal a complex, but reasonably workable, structure for controlling prices which did not obviously lead to economic distortion, and which might therefore—with suitable modifications—endure for quite a long time without doing too much violence to a free enterprise system. This was not much appreciated at the time, but in retrospect it is of crucial importance (though whether for good or ill is hard to say). Three years later, despite sea-changes almost everywhere else in the politico-economic system, the Price Commission and the price code were still in business under a Labour Government and still grudgingly accepted by industry. This was in sharp contrast to the situation in the George Brown era, when one of Whitehall's problems was its lack of any mechanism for long-term price control which would not lead to crude and unacceptable distortions in the allocation of national resources.

Phase 2 worked reasonably well, but trouble started for the government when the time came to replace it by Phase 3 in October 1973. Somewhere during the spring and summer of 1973 the process of consultation between government and TUC slipped—not through any overt design or conflict, but through inattention by government.

Once again, foreign distractions may have provided part of the reason for this. Following the Yom Kippur War between Egypt, Syria and Israel, the Arab oil-producing countries began a selective ban on oil exports to Western states, threatening to throw their economies into chaos. For a time it seemed as if the whole postwar economic structure was in jeopardy. During the autumn the ban was relaxed until it disappeared entirely, but it was replaced by a fourfold rise in oil prices imposed by the Organisation of Petroleum Exporting Countries (OPEC). What had begun as a means to apply political pressure in the Arab cause became instead a highly successful producers' cartel pushing up world prices.

The effect was to transform, at least for a time, the economic balance of world power, pushing the Western economies into heavy external deficit and syphoning off vast amounts of purchasing power into the oil-producing states. During the subsequent three years the balance of trade was to be at least partly restored, owing to a quite unexpected propensity to spend their newly acquired wealth on capital development and conspicuous consumption on the part of the Middle Eastern countries constituting the core of OPEC. But the necessary shift into exports of a greater part of national production in the Western countries meant that less was available for other forms of spending; and, more seriously, the very sharp rise in oil prices gave domestic inflation a major new fillip, completely negating the attempts to control it by internal measures of restraint. All the Western countries were affected in greater or lesser degree by this new tidal wave of inflation, not least the UK.

CONFRONTATION WITH THE MINERS

In the UK the oil crisis had a further, special dimension. The miners' wage agreement was due for renewal at the end of 1973, and it became clear during the summer that the union was in a militant mood, and that the negotiations would pose major difficulties if they were not to be allowed to break the pay code. The TUC was given the impression that Phase 3 would be constructed in such a way as to provide a loophole for an exceptional increase for the miners. Clearly the oil crisis had enormously strengthened their bargaining power and could be said to make them a special case.

In the event Phase 3, introduced in October 1973, did not seem to contain the flexibility needed to satisfy the miners without breaching the policy. It stipulated a new wage norm of 7% (or a flat rate of £2.25 a week for lower-paid workers), with certain extras available for sorting out anomalies, rewarding merit, compensating for the higher cost of living in London and the unpleasantness of working 'unsocial' hours, etc. Most importantly, it introduced the principle of a 'threshold' agreement. If the retail price index rose by 7% above its October level during the ensuing twelve months, workers would be entitled to an automatic wage rise in compensation; the formula ensured a 1.2% rise in wages for every 1% rise in prices above the threshold. Price controls remained virtually as in Phase 2. The government believed that these controls, given a productivity increase of 3-4%, would keep prices below the threshold. In fact the threshold was reached in April 1974, and by the time the agreement was terminated (in autumn 1975) no fewer than twelve threshold increments had become payable, amounting to an extra £4.80 a week per worker. The threshold approach is not likely to commend itself to future governments in an inflationary situation.

This is not to say, of course, that the principle of indexation of wages and, for that matter, other forms of income—i.e., linking them formally with movements in prices—is wrong or impracticable. In fact in an inflationary situation it is hard to resist some form of indexation, if only because by this means one can take some of the 'anticipatory' element out of wage demands—as well as doing something to protect the weaker from the socially divisive ravages of inflation. But the formula chosen by the British in 1973 turned out, in the special circumstances of the time (with inflation further fuelled by the explosion in oil prices), to be in itself highly inflationary. For this reason, perhaps unjustly, it tended to discredit the concept.

Thus, as the government approached its crucial confrontation with the miners' union, the links established with the TUC leaders during the previous year had been allowed to weaken, and the TUC felt no commitment towards Phase 3. The union rejected a pay offer from the National Coal Board which would have given them a 13% increase, and which seemed to exploit all the available loopholes in Phase 3, and imposed a ban on overtime working. Various behind-the-scenes efforts at mediation between government and union failed to resolve the deadlock, and the nation's coal stocks began to dip dangerously as winter drew on. In desperation, the government announced drastic cuts in consumption to take effect on 1 January 1974. The bulk of industry was ordered to go onto a three-day week to conserve energy, and there were severe cuts in public electricity consumption involving a partial black-out and other measures. The country seemed to be back in the wartime atmosphere of the early 1940s, with its industrial economy visibly running down and a grey austerity everywhere.

As the miners maintained the overtime ban and drew up plans for a ballot on a national strike, the TUC tried ineffectually to intervene. On 9 January, at a meeting of the NEDC, the TUC members indicated that, if the government could facilitate a deal between the Coal Board and the miners, other unions would not use this as an argument in negotiations on their own settlements. If genuine, this offer met the government's main concern over a settlement with the miners—namely, that any settlement would set a precedent for other unions, and thus destroy Phase 3. But the government either misunderstood or mistrusted what the TUC was saying, and the offer was not taken up.

During January the country drifted steadily towards economic breakdown and a fatal confrontation between government and unions. There was a total impasse in the negotiations. Political fever ran high. The question of the governability of Britain was in question. The government suspected that the miners' action was politically motivated, an attempt to destroy a democratically elected government. Some unwise remarks by the deputy president of the union, a Communist, lent substance to this belief, which was in fact almost certainly false. Had it been true, it would have been clearly counter-productive, for the evidence of the public opinion polls at the time indicated that if the government had gone to the country in a general election on the issue of 'Who governs Britain?' it would have won an overwhelming majority.

Not surprisingly, many voices in the Tory Party were urging the Prime Minister to do just this, as the only way of breaking the deadlock and saving the country. But there was one drawback. Whichever party won the election, the new government would still have to negotiate with the miners, who were now preparing for a strike while the government was preparing for an election.

Edward Heath himself was in two minds. He saw the advantages of an election, but at the same time he wanted desperately to unite and not further to divide the nation. He hesitated, and was lost. The election was not called until February, by which time the mood of the nation had moved from fury at the miners to criticism of the government's mishandling of the situation.[3] And instead of tackling the issue of the governability of Britain head-on, Heath fought a low-key, restrained campaign focused on the need for moderation and national unity, but failing to answer the question of how he would solve the miners' dispute if he won.

So against all the odds, the election was lost—narrowly but decisively. Heath was replaced as Prime Minister by Harold Wilson, in circumstances of national division and catastrophe greater than at any time since the Suez fiasco nearly twenty years earlier. Looking back on that period of chaos and passion, what strikes one most was the almost total breakdown in communications between the various people and groups whose job was to help run the country, and a resulting attribution of sinister motives whereas in fact all concerned were under the malign domination of the great god Muddle.[4] The government was out of touch with the TUC, which in turn was out of touch with the miners. The moderate leadership in the miners' union led the government to believe that they could secure a settlement which in the event they could not deliver. The Coal Board mishandled the negotiations in the early stages. Worst of all, Heath was isolated from his own Cabinet colleagues, so that the expert advice which would normally be coming through the Whitehall machine—notably from the Department of Employment—was either unavailable to, or ignored by, him and his closest advisers.

If this book has a tragic hero, it must be Edward Heath—the Peel of the present-day Conservative Party. Like Peel with the Corn Laws, he became converted halfway through his term of office to a policy which was at odds with the instincts of his colleagues and with the recognised party objectives, and like Peel he became isolated from his followers, and paid for it with the loss of office and leadership. Within twelve months of his election defeat, Heath was forced to contest the leadership of his party in the Commons and was defeated. He withdrew to the back benches. As with Peel, his problems were compounded by a shyness which made it difficult for him to communicate effectively. But he remains nevertheless a major figure in the British political landscape.

'INDUSTRIAL REVIEW TO 1977'

After the turmoil and turbulence which attended the fall of the Heath Government, it is a relief to turn for a moment—before resuming the narrative of 1974—to an episode of at least relative sanity and calm, though it had little enough influence on national affairs.

In January 1972 the Neddy Council asked the Office to look at the major industrial problems and changes likely to arise for the nation's key industrial sectors over the next five years, particularly in the context of entry into the EEC. As with *The Task Ahead*, much of the stimulus seems to have come from the CBI and TUC. This was the origin of the *Industrial Review to 1977*, approved by the Council in the summer of 1973.[5]

The review covered agriculture and eleven manufacturing industries which together accounted for some 60% of UK manufacturing output.[6] It was based on two alternative assumptions of GDP growth—3½% and 5% per annum (the higher figure put in at the insistence of the TUC). The review, which unlike the National Plan and *The Task Ahead* was under the direction of the NEDO and not the government, was carried out in five stages. First, the changing composition of demand for the various industries' products in the UK market; then assessments of changes in exports and imports resulting from EEC entry and other changes in the international environment; estimates of changes in the composition of UK output which would be needed to meet this expected pattern of demand; manpower and investment requirements; and, finally, an examination of the problems and opportunities that would be created for each industry, and ways of meeting them. In all five stages the EDCs and industry working parties were involved.

The macro component of this planning exercise was minimal. The growth projections on which it was based were avowedly purely illustrative. (There was also an assumption that world trade would grow by 10% per annum.) The review was more industrially oriented than any of its predecessors, and also the one which went farthest in recognising that British industry operated in an international and not just a domestic market. Besides the EEC question, there was the likely effect of negotiations for tariff cuts in the GATT (General Agreement on Trade and Tariffs) and the trend towards international specialisation.

The results of the exercise were not terribly exciting. There were no major recommendations for government. The general impression that emerged was that resources would by and large be adequate to sustain the 3½% growth rate, while the implications of 5% growth were not in all cases properly assessed (few outside the TUC took this assumption seriously). More investment would be needed even for 3½% growth in chemicals and castings, but there seemed no overwhelming reason why it should not be forthcoming. Manpower was not seen as a major constraint on 3½% growth. Research showed that despite the difficulties of the previous five years there had been a significant underlying improvement in the productivity of both labour and capital, and there was no apparent reason why this should not continue.

The unexciting nature of the review's conclusions should not disguise the fact that the industrial analysis was much more thorough than in the past, and therefore of more real potential use to government. For the first time government was getting through the NEDO and the EDCs effective feedback from the industrial sectors. This was a basis on which future planning operations could be built. But the tendency to underestimate import propensity remained, and this would have weakened the use of the review even had it not been overtaken by events even more rapidly than some of its predecessors.

For once again the planners had been unlucky in their timing. One month after the review was published the oil crisis broke on an unprepared

Western world, and all the projections became outdated overnight. Such are the hazards of prediction.

### 1974: THE YEAR OF TRAUMA

Harold Wilson had not expected to win the February 1974 election. He did so by the narrowest of margins. For the first time since the war no party emerged from the election with an overall majority. Labour, as the party with the largest number of seats, formed a minority government.[7] As in 1964, it was generally accepted that another election would need to be held at the earliest opportunity to clarify the situation, and the country continued to function in a pre-election atmosphere.

Labour had spent a bleak four years in opposition, trying to heal the wounds inflicted on party unity during its period in office. Both the trade unions and the constituency parties had moved sharply to the left in the late sixties and early seventies. Like Edward Heath, Harold Wilson had deeply offended some of the basic instincts of his party during his period of office, in particular by two measures, both of which ironically proved abortive: the attempt to enter the EEC and the attempt to legislate on trade unions and industrial relations. Both measures had subsequently been carried through by the Tories.

The rift on Europe was healed by a formula which would require a Labour Government to re-negotiate Britain's terms of entry into the Community and then submit the results to a national referendum. This pledge was duly carried out, and the referendum held in mid-1975 produced an overwhelming endorsement of the UK's continued membership of the EEC, much to the discomfiture of the Left. But the split between the political and industrial wings of the Labour movement opened up by *In Place of Strife* was potentially harder to heal.

The task was facilitated, however, by the confrontation policy adopted by the Heath Government up to mid-1972 *vis-à-vis* the unions. This enabled the Labour Party to champion an alternative approach, based on a recognition of the fact that power had shifted dramatically towards the unions and their members, as a result of the pressures of democracy in a technologically complex society and the fact of union monopoly bargaining power; the shift was evidenced, not only by the fact that wage inflation had intensified at the end of the 1960s in all the main industrial countries despite mounting unemployment—which, according to orthodox Keynesian theory, should have weakened trade union bargaining power[8]; but also by the ability of the union movement, in the UK at any rate, to negate the effect of any legislation it did not like. Not only had the unions prevented a Labour Government from legislating. By refusing to co-operate they had effectively rendered the Conservatives' Industrial Relations Act a dead letter.

The most dramatic evidence of this occurred during the February 1974 election, when the CBI director-general Campbell Adamson was quoted as having said, in what he believed was an off-the-record meeting, that the Act had sullied industrial relations at all levels and should be repealed. Edward Heath—almost certainly wrongly—considered that this remark, which was widely reported, cost him the election.

This analysis was of course much easier for Labour to accept than for the Conservatives. It enabled the party to project itself as the protagonist of consensus as against confrontation, and as the party which could best manage the unions. This image, carefully cultivated, was to stand it in good stead over the next few years.

SOCIAL CONTRACT AND PLANNING AGREEMENTS

The new approach was built around the so-called 'Social Contract', negotiated between the two wings of the Labour movement before the 1974 election, and subsequently renewed periodically. The main elements of the contract, of which Mr Wedgwood Benn—reappointed Secretary of State for Industry in 1974—can lay claim to being the main architect, were as follows.

On labour relations, Labour pledged itself to abolish the Industrial Relations Act, and replace it by legislation which strengthened the position of the unions, gave workers greater job security, removed discrimination against women in employment, and moved towards greater participation of worker representatives in decision making in large enterprises and greater industrial democracy. These moves made major inroads into the traditional prerogatives of management, which had hitherto been maintained more strongly in the UK than for example in West Germany, Scandinavia or the Netherlands.

On prices and incomes, Labour broadly maintained the Conservative policy on price control, while abolishing the Pay Board (whose first and last chairman was the luckless Sir Frank Figgures, who had been succeeded as NEDO director-general in 1973 by Sir Ronald McIntosh), [9] and Phase 3 in so far as it applied to pay. Food subsidies were introduced to help keep down prices. The TUC undertook to exercise restraint on wages, in return for the abolition of statutory wage control. This enabled the miners' claim to be settled swiftly but expensively (the increases ranged from £6.71 to £16.31 a week), so that power supplies and industrial working could return to normal.

The other main elements of the social contract dealt with social policy—on which a number of expensive commitments were made—and policies of industrial intervention, which were enshrined in a White Paper, *The Regeneration of British Industry*, published by Wedgwood Benn in 1974. This Paper, which foreshadowed a third Industry Act to reinforce those of 1968 and 1972, provided for the establishment of a new body, the National Enterprise Board, and planning agreements between individual enterprises and the state.

Before describing these new measures in detail, it is necessary to say a little about the background of fact and theory from which they sprang. First, the facts. The industrial fabric had been gravely battered by the inflation, aggravated by price control, industrial unrest and the disruption of the three-day week. It was evident that some other major industrial companies were lkely to follow Rolls-Royce into bankruptcy. (Those which in fact did so, or which needed rescue operations during 1974 and 1975, included British Leyland, Ferranti, Alfred Herbert, Harland and Wolff and the British operations of Chrysler.) The need for measures to prop up the private sector was evident. It was also, of course, attractive to the strategists of the Left, who saw it as a major opportunity of boosting the state sector of the economy, on the lines of the IRI (*Istituto per la Ricotruzione Industriale*) in Italy.

There was also a good deal of cynicism on the Left, headed by Wedgwood Benn, about Neddy and sector planning, on the reasonable grounds that such planning does not necessarily commit the decision makers in industry. The idea, which as we have seen was not entirely absent during the 1964-70 period, of direct negotiations between major firms and the government on planning commitments, began therefore to play a large part in Labour thinking while in Opposition. It was well known that in France such agreements had been commonplace for some time, and it was thought that part of France's economic success sprang from the way in which governments were able to steer resources towards the most worthy recipients on the basis of firm-state planning agreements (which also ensured that the firms behaved in the way the state wanted).

However, there was a major innovation in Labour's approach to planning agreements which rendered them much more offensive to industry. The Wedgwood Benn approach envisaged a third party to the planning agreement—the workers, represented by their union officials or shop stewards; this was in line with the basic concept of the social contract, that power had not only shifted significantly away from management towards the shopfloor, but that it should be encouraged to do so further. (We shall analyse this concept further in the next chapter.)

Thus the Benn White Paper combined two concepts which had always hitherto been kept separate, in Britain and on the Continent. One objective was to give government the power to provide selective aid to enterprises or industrial sectors in difficulties, and to intervene in the decision making of the private sector where the national interest required. The other was to give a powerful push towards industrial democracy in the sense of power sharing within the enterprise.

During 1974, therefore, the Labour Government proceeded to implement the social contract. The economy moved forward again, and the social ferment of the beginning of the year subsided. But the cost was heavy, in terms of inflation. Rightly or wrongly, the feeling was abroad that the green light had been given to inflationary wage demands. Weekly wage rates, which had risen by 9% in 1970, 13% in 1971, 14% in 1972, 15½% in 1973, jumped by 26% in 1974. Britain's inflation rate doubled during the year, and moved ahead of all other major industrial countries except for Italy and Japan (the two countries hardest hit by the oil price rise).

In the world economy 1974 saw the onset of the worst postwar recession. The downturn, triggered off by the oil price rise, affected all the major industrial countries. The UK was to some extent shielded from the recession during 1974 by the sharp rise in wages, which boosted internal spending, and still more by the very heavy rate of public spending. Firms in both the public and the private sector were discouraged from laying off workers, and government money was piped in lavishly to prop up ailing private sector enterprises. The consequence was that the UK's external competitiveness worsened and the balance of payments went further still into the red. Though prices rose sharply, they did not keep pace with wages, so that industry once again found its profits squeezed. In these circumstances investment was sharply cut, and firms struggled to survive in the worst cash squeeze in more than thirty years.

A second election in October marginally strengthened Labour's position. It won eighteen more seats, and had a nominal majority of three over all other parties. Superficially this was exactly the same situation that Labour had had in the Parliament following the October 1964 election, when Harold Wilson formed his first government; but in fact the government's position was stronger now, because of the greater fragmentation of the opposition. Nevertheless the parliamentary majority remained fragile and precarious.

By the end of the year wage settlements of 30% or more were becoming normal, and the economy was showing the symptoms of a South American banana republic. Despite higher taxes, the state was finding its resources heavily stretched to meet both its social commitments and the costs of subsidising the weaker parts of the private sector. Public indebtedness was growing alarmingly. Clearly a change of course was required. It came in mid-1975, almost as dramatically as the Tories' U-turn three years before.

It was clear that within the Labour government two schools of thought were contending. The Left, led by Wedgwood Benn, wanted to meet the crisis by further *dirigisme*, by extending the state's umbrella further to cover the defective parts of the private sector, by withdrawing from the EEC and protecting the balance of payments by import controls: in short, by maintaining a socialist siege economy.

Part of the Left's blueprint was spelt out in the 1975 Industry Bill, which was to put into effect the proposals in *The Regeneration of British Industry*. The Bill, as published at the start of 1975, envisaged the establishment of a National Enterprise Board (NEB), with capital of more than £1,000 million (seven times more than the IRC had had) to take over the government's shareholdings in private industry, and with powers to invest in the private sector at its own initiative or at the state's behest. The NEB thus had much more power, as well as much more money, than the IRC. The IRC's function was to effect a merger or rationalisation and then pull out. The NEB was envisaged as having a continuing managing function in those sectors where it intervened.

Second, the Bill envisaged a programme of planning agreements between the government and selected large firms, at which their plans for the coming years were to be disclosed to and discussed with (and presumably then modified and monitored by) government.

While the powers proposed for the government in the Industry Bill were wide, it was apparent that the proposals were less radical than in the previous White Paper.[10] The National Enterprise Board had more sharply delimited terms of reference, and its boss, Lord Ryder, would report to the Prime Minister and not to Mr Benn. More important, planning agreements were to be voluntary rather than mandatory, and the participation of the workers' representatives in them was minimised. They were to be seen as an adjunct to sector planning, not a substitute for it. It was clear that the Left was starting to lose ground within the Cabinet.

BACK FROM THE BRINK

The crucial event in 1975, however, was the May referendum on the EEC. Uniquely, the Cabinet split publicly on the issue, with a small group of ministers headed by Messrs Benn and Shore joining with the TUC to recommend rejection of the re-negotiated terms of membership and Britain's withdrawal from the Community. The Cabinet collectively, on the other hand, endorsed the terms and recommended their acceptance, and the Prime Minister and Foreign Secretary campaigned actively for Britain to stay inside the EEC. The referendum produced a majority of more than two to one in favour of staying in—a decisive setback for the Left, and incidentally for the TUC. Though the activities of the rebels were publicly condoned, Mr Wilson took the opportunity to move Mr Benn from the key Department of Industry and to replace him with the more middle-of-the-road Mr Eric Varley (whose former post as Minister for Energy went to Mr Benn—a Wilsonian 'swap' reminiscent of those involving Messrs Stewart and Brown, and Jenkins and Callaghan, in his previous administration).

Thus it fell to Eric Varley to pilot the Industry Bill through Parliament, and in the course of its passage the role and importance of planning agreements suffered a further dilution. The change of personalities at the Department of Industry led to a much closer relationship with the Treasury, which was to have important consequences for the evolution of industrial strategy and it produced an immediate improvement in relations between government and CBI.

Events moved swiftly after the referendum result. Some of the TUC leaders—notably Mr Jack Jones, general secretary of the transport and general workers (TGWU)—had become convinced by the summer of 1975 that a measure of wage restraint was essential for political and economic reasons; without it inflation would run riot and the government would be forced out of office. During this period, therefore, the TUC began to distance itself from the 'alternative strategy' propounded by the Left—especially after the referendum result had discredited one plank of that strategy. The alliance forged between the Left and the big unions in the aftermath of *In Place of Strife*, which had dominated the Labour movement for six years, was falling apart under the stresses of power. In July the government was able to reach agreement with the TUC on a new pay policy, based on an increase of not more than £6 a week for all workers earning up to £8,500 a year, and nothing for anybody earning over that figure, for the next twelve months. This was supposed to equate roughly to an average 10% increase. But it discriminated heavily in favour of the low paid, eroding differentials and moving the whole pay structure in a more egalitarian direction. At the higher levels it led to a number of distortions and anomalies, and a considerable amount of managerial frustration. (There was also an explicit exemption from the policy for wage increases designed to achieve the statutory requirement of equal pay for women doing the same jobs as men.)

The policy was crude, but it reflected widely held instincts about social justice in Britain—and it worked. It was overwhelmingly endorsed by the TUC at its annual Congress in September, and for the first time in postwar British history a voluntary policy of wage restraint endorsed by the trade union movement was adhered to throughout its duration virtually without exception. Moreover, during the twelve months when the £6-a-week policy was in force the number of days lost by strikes in British industry dropped to a twenty-two-year low. Those who argued that the acceptance of TUC power would bring with it acceptance by the TUC of responsibility,[11] could claim for the first time some evidence to support their faith.

A number of factors were combining to push the government back towards the kind of tripartism represented by the NEDC. In the heady climate of early 1974 Neddy's role looked almost as marginal as it had after the Tory victory of 1970. Planning agreements, *dirigisme* and interventionism were in, it seemed; tripartism, national and sector planning and consensus were out. The TUC had acquired an unchallenged power and prestige. It had brought down one government; it was courted, consulted and fawned on by its successor. It was dictating national policy without having to accept any reciprocal constraints or obligations.

By contrast the CBI was shell-shocked and demoralised. Its responsibility to the national interest reflected in its unilateral price initiative had apparently gone unrewarded. It had had to suffer the privations of the three-day week for nothing. Worst of all, its director-general was (quite unfairly) suspected of having helped Labour to win the election. The government hardly bothered to consult it. Not surprisingly, the CBI experienced a right-wing backlash from a powerful section of its membership during 1974 which severely limited its ability to contribute to the national debate.

But, in fact, as could have been predicted, the tide was moving back in its favour; for, just as Edward Heath had found he could not govern effectively against the opposition of the TUC, so the Labour Government found that it needed a certain measure of industrial support if it was to have any economic success; for, in our mixed economy, it is after all the directors and managers of the private enterprise sector who overwhelmingly determine what exports will take place and what productive investment will be undertaken.

What is also interesting, and testifies in a sense to the vitality of the Neddy structure, is that direct informal contacts between the CBI and the TUC to concert views on certain NEDC agenda items have taken place over a number of years. These meetings, held in conditions of some secrecy, were suspended during the furore over the Industrial Relations Act, but resumed in 1973. In April 1975 they led to a joint paper to the NEDC calling for a return to indicative planning, with macro forecasts provided by the Treasury and detailed sector forecasts prepared by the EDCs.

The TUC-CBI paper chimed in with the government's wish to take advantage of the breathing space won by the pay agreement to get the economy on to a sounder basis. Though the internal climate had been greatly improved by the new realism of the unions, the objective indicators could hardly be worse. While the inflation rate was starting to come down in most of the industrial Western world, in the UK it had yet to peak, as past wage rises were fed through to prices. Moreover, the attempt to buy off unemployment through state subsidies had been largely abandoned owing to its prohibitive cost, and the unemployment rate was starting to rise ominously. The UK was experiencing the full force of the world recession at a time when some other countries were already starting to pull out of it, and when our cost structure was becoming steadily more uncompetitive. Company profitability had fallen in real terms from around 10% return on capital in the 1960s to about 2%. For this and other reasons, investment was flat.

THE NEW INDUSTRIAL STRATEGY

So any move which might help us to break out of the squirrel-cage was welcome. Discussions at the NEDC led to a special meeting at Chequers on 5 November which agreed a White Paper on *An Approach to Industrial Strategy*. This document, reproduced in full in Appendix 7, set out a new pattern of economic planning to be carried out through the Neddy machinery. More than this, it officially reinstated tripartism. Government and TUC explicitly recognised the necessity for profits as a basis for industrial investment, and the need to avoid pouring public money into enterprises or sectors which had no hope of long-term viability. (Unfortunately industry's delight was somewhat abated when, shortly afterwards, the government seemed to break its good resolutions by agreeing to subsidise the loss-making British subsidiary of Chrysler, despite an internal Whitehall report which indicated that the motor industry had excess capacity.)

The White Paper emphasised the combination of long-term and short-term problems facing the UK, reflecting 'the relative decline of British industry which has been continuous for many years', and which could not be put right overnight. It stressed the need for a new strategic framework within which individual measures could be planned. Such a strategic framework was needed, not just as a guide to the best use of the various weapons in the government's own armoury (the NEB is explicitly mentioned in this context) but also for manpower planning.[12] The need for a redeployment of labour from declining to expanding industries was recognised, and there must be effective planning for mobility, training and re-training.

In a brief inventory of the main reasons for the UK's poor performance, the White Paper listed: low investment, inefficient use of capital, poor choice of investment; low labour productivity resulting from faults both of management and labour, inadequate national manpower policies, negative attitudes towards productivity and mobility; too frequent changes of policy by successive governments making it difficult for companies to plan ahead, pre-emption of resources by the public sector and by personal consumption, government intervention in nationalised industries' pricing, investment and employment policies; declining industrial profitability, imperfections in the capital markets, a capital market which did not give priority to the needs of industry. An attack would have to be made on all these areas if the UK was to become a high-growth, high-wage, high-output fully employed economy.

Thus any national industrial strategy must involve better co-ordination of policies, based on a good information feedback from individual firms and sectors; more effective use of the instruments of industrial policy and the deployment of financial aid to industry; more effective manpower policies; and an adequate rate of financial return for the productive sector. Above all, 'we must get away from policies of confrontation, and work together in the national interest towards agreed objectives'.

How was this to be done? First, the government would give priority, over the next few years, to policies encouraging industrial investment at the expense of private and public consumption, including the social services. A switch of resources towards investment and exports had to be made as the country began to expand its economy again.[13] The government would also have to ensure the effective co-ordination of macro- and micro-economic policies.

On a technical level, the White Paper posed the alternative of a new National Plan, but rejected it.

The likelihood is that any plan which erected a single complete and mutually consistent set of industrial forecasts and targets would rapidly be falsified by events and have to be discarded. This would once again discredit the process of industrial planning in this country as did previous attempts, which failed largely because they were based on unsustainable economic assumptions, and paid too little attention

to the constraints affecting individual industries and companies ...
This time a more flexible approach is proposed. We aim to provide
a framework in which to consider the likely prospects of the
most important sectors of industry over a period of five or more
years ahead and to indicate their role in meeting our overall economic
objectives.

One of the most important elements in this new-style planning would
be the identification of the key sectors for future national growth. These
would be the industries which on past performance and current prospects
seemed intrinsically likely to be successful; those which had the potential
for success if the right actions were taken; and those whose performance
was most important to the rest of industry (such as key component
suppliers).

Thus there would be sector plans or strategies related to national
medium-term growth assumptions provided by government. Targets
would be set for the individual sectors, and the whole exercise would be
updated annually, in such a way that the Chancellor could take into
account the recommendations of the sector working parties in framing
his budget.

In the event the industrial strategy was to prove rather less selective,
rather more indiscriminate, than the original presentation indicated.
Government had indicated its intention of 'backing winners', and by
implication of allowing 'losers' to fend for themselves, and if need be
sink without trace. But this was easier said than done, at a time when
there was general concern about employment levels—and when government's confidence in its ability actually to identify 'winners' was less than
complete.

Following the Chequers meeting, the NEDO set up thirty-nine separate
sector working parties, operating on the same tripartite basis as the
EDCs.[14] Some of these working parties were coterminous with the
EDCs, some were sub-groups of bigger EDCs, some were outside the
EDC framework altogether.[15] These groups had to draw up the first
stage of the industrial strategy. Separate working groups were set up to
deal with manpower and financial questions. The exercise was master-
minded by a steering group representing government, CBI, TUC and
NEDO.

On the government side, the key departments were the Treasury and
the Department of Industry. A quite new development was the personal
importance attached to the exercise by the Chancellor, Mr Denis Healey.
At his insistence the Treasury established for the first time its own
Industrial Policy Department under a deputy secretary, Mr Alan Lord.
Mr Lord was the chairman of the steering group, though much of the
detailed expertise came of course from the Industry Department representatives. For the first time, the Whitehall machine seemed to have
geared itself to integrate economic and industrial policy in a meaningful
and sensible way. The role which the DEA had tried and failed to

perform ten years before had been absorbed into the decision-making process of the established ministries.

The new style of planning was to be less numerical, less comprehensive, more oriented to objectives, issues, constraints and opportunities than previous plans. It was to build from the bottom up, rather than the top down. To this extent it accorded much more closely with the views of industry than had been the case in the past. In the 1960s the CBI had persistently asked that the planners should begin by finding out what industry thinks, before telling industry what government thought. Even *The Task Ahead*, though better than the National Plan from industry's point of view, did not go far enough in this direction. The new industrial strategy approach went much farther.

Moreover, industry itself in its corporate planning was moving away from detailed, highly quantitative forecasts towards more policy-oriented strategy plans; partly no doubt because of the havoc caused to financial forecasts by inflation. To this extent, also, the industrial strategy approach was in line with the broad trend of business thinking.

The thirty-nine sector working parties were due to report to the NEDC in July 1976. In the intervening eight months the economy began slowly to pick up from the recession—more slowly than most of the rest of the industrial world. Inflation started to fall, at about the same rate as, but from a higher base than, our main overseas competitors. The Chancellor in his April Budget made some cautious moves to stimulate investment, and was generally seen to be following the Chequers mandate. There was a sharp quarrel with the TUC, who felt that the government was cutting public spending unnecessarily fiercely at a time when there was still severe unemployment, and when the private sector could still not absorb all the resources (including especially workers) released from the public sector. The Chancellor, however, stuck to his guns. (Indeed, he had no option, for Britain was in need of foreign loans to roll over her existing debts, and a reduction in public sector borrowing was a pre-condition for such loans; Britain's external indebtedness had indeed reached frightening proportions.)

Despite this fracas, agreement was reached remarkably easily with the TUC on the next stage of counter-inflation policy to replace the £6-a-week freeze in July 1976. The basis of Stage 2 was a wage increase ceiling for most workers of 4½%—substantially less than the expected rise in prices. Workers earning over £8,500 a year could get increases of up to £4 a week.[16] There was some easing in the highly complex provisions of the price code. The new pay policy was in fact tougher than the previous one, and still heavily egalitarian in its implications, though a little more flexible in details than its predecessor. Debate was already beginning to focus on whether, when Stage 2 expired in July 1977, there would be a Stage 3—and if so, how much more flexibility (especially for the higher-paid worker) could be incorporated while still retaining the necessary restraint and the politically desirable element of social justice. There was general agreement among the NEDC partners that some element of pay restraint would be needed probably up to 1980 or beyond to ensure that the UK remained competitive, but there were considerable doubts as to whether this would be politically possible.

The first stage of the industrial strategy was unveiled in July 1976, when the NEDC considered and approved reports from thirty-seven of the sector working parties (two of them—bearings and gears—were not yet ready) and from the special committee set up under Sir Eric Roll on finance for industry,[17] together with papers on agriculture and distribution, and a rather disappointing one on manpower problems from the Department of Employment and the Manpower Services Commission. The NEDC meeting was chaired by the new Prime Minister, James Callaghan, Harold Wilson having recently resigned.

These reports had been drawn up without any macro-economic framework. The sector groups were asked to make their own macro assumptions; so, although their field covered some 60% of manufacturing industry, their reports could not be aggregated to form a national picture. In any case, what they had been asked to do was to examine their position in world markets, to try to assess their competitiveness and how it could be improved, and what constraints were likely to affect their performance in the expected upswing phase of the economy.

The sector working party reports were very detailed. The main recommendations concerned possible bottlenecks in the near to medium future. Possible constraints were identified in the field of supplies—the need for better maker-user relations was stressed—manpower and finance. There were a number of complaints about the price code and its effect on profitablity, and thus investment.

The government was able to point to the investment incentives already provided: the 100% depreciation allowance on investment in plant and machinery; the special regional investment incentives; and the sector schemes for new investment in wool textiles, ferrous foundries, machine tools and clothing, to which paper and board were about to be added. The NEB was also financing a special stockbuilding scheme for machine tools, to complement the stockpiling scheme already in operation for steel.

On the question of finance for industry, the Roll working group presented an interim report which reached the unsurprising conclusion that the main problem was the low profitability of industry, and its reluctance to borrow at current rates. A number of specific points about company finance raised in the sector reports were being studied further by this working group, whose remit was to discover gaps which could be plugged in the City-industry relationship.[18] Some specific issues regarding export finance were also raised in the sector reports.

On manpower, the main concerns were a possible lack of skilled labour as demand recovered, and specific shortages of qualified scientists and engineers. Some of the sectors recommended action on overmanning and low labour productivity.

Most of the sector reports recommended more effort and resources to be devoted to product development, and to improving international marketing. There was concern over delivery delays in some sectors, and a general view that government could use its public purchasing to help industry improve its overall performance.

Most of the points raised in the sector reports had a familiar look about them. Many were the same ones as had featured in the Orange Book and the National Plan. Nevertheless, the check-list of action required was much more detailed and precise than in previous exercises, and most of the reports had a practical, down-to-earth air about them. It was agreed that there would be regular progress reports on the actions in the check-list, and that by January 1977 the sector working groups should be asked to agree targets for overseas market penetration (this might pose problems of adequacy of the statistical data base in some cases); and there should be a review of the main constraints in time for the Chancellor to take them into account in framing his 1977 Budget. Plainly Mr Healey had in mind the possibility of more selective measures to help particular sectors, at a time of necessary restraint in overall public spending.

One refreshing feature of the whole exercise was the general acceptance that the relevant market was a world one and not the domestic market, and the overwhelming importance of building up overseas sales. No doubt one of the factors behind this was the decline of sterling relative to most foreign currencies, which greatly affected the relative profitability of overseas to home business.

The NEDC meeting was by no means all sweetness and light. Some of the TUC members thought they detected an undue amount of political lobbying in some of the sector reports. The CBI members were concerned about the viability of sector targets—how far could they commit individual firms?—and sensitive to the charge that industry was not investing enough. The TUC emphasis on boosting employment and the CBI concern for raising profitability were not easily reconcilable. However, in the end a consensus was reached, and it was agreed that the sectors should be kept under constant review and a further full-scale report made in fifteen months, and that a determined attempt should be made to publicise their findings throughout their industries.

The following month the Chancellor presented the Treasury's medium-term economic forecast—the macro component of the planning exercise. As in the past, the forecast contained two hypotheses—a projection based on past trends and existing policies, and a more optimistic 'target' projection. For the first time, the government forecast took the business cycle into account, and did not simply project trend growth-rates. The lower end of the forecast 'wedge' predicted a GDP rise of about 3½% a year to 1980—4½% over the next eighteen months, and 2¼% thereafter; this would still leave unacceptably large numbers of people unemployed by the end of the decade. The alternative scenario featured a GDP rise of 4½-5½% per annum up to 1980, with an unprecedentedly high increase in manufacturing output throughout the period of 8% a year.

Faced with these alternatives, the Council passed a unanimous resolution (the first in Neddy's history) that the first scenario was unacceptable, and that all efforts must therefore be concentrated on achieving the second alternative. The CBI indicated that it was hoping to bring its own 'Programme for National Recovery'—subsequently published under the title *The Road to Recovery*—before the Council in October.

Thus, as the nation's leaders prepared to set off for their August holidays in the torrid summer of 1976, it was clear that they had moved closer than for many years past towards a consensus on the overall objectives of a national economic/industrial strategy for recovery, and a joint determination to. improve the nation's economic performance. What was less clear was how far that determination would go towards taking the many gritty and unpleasant measures which would be needed to implement the strategy, and whether the ground lost over the previous two decades could be recovered in time to avert a further, perhaps catastrophic, relapse. To provide even a tentative answer to these questions one must look beyond the kissing ring of national leaders assembled round Neddy's top table in Millbank Tower, to their varied constituents in the real and troubled world outside.[19]

## NOTES

1 The story of the Conservatives' Industrial Relations Act was a sad one. Based largely on *In Place of Strife*, it relied on trade union co-operation through the device of registration. In order to retain the benefits of friendly society status, trade unions were required to register under the Act and thus render themselves liable to its disciplines. The TUC voted to suspend any member-union which registered, and in fact very few did so. There was virtually total non-observance of the Act by the trade unions, and in these circumstances it proved impossible to enforce. There were various confrontations between lawyers and trade unions leading to heavy fines on unions for non-compliance with the Act; these were annulled when the Act was repealed by the Labour Government in 1974. There were worse difficulties when unofficial strikers were jailed, and promptly became martyrs. Various legal subterfuges had to be found to get them out of prison because of the disproportionately serious effect their detention was having on industrial relations. The various legal institutions set up under the Act to introduce the rule of law into industrial relations were all dissolved in 1974. A decade of debate and legislation on what had been recognised, ever since the Donovan Commission was set up, as one of Britain's gravest industrial weaknesses had achieved nothing, except to demonstrate the power of the unions, and to bring the law into discredit.

2 Edward Heath had won his political spurs as Britain's chief negotiator with the Europeans in Harold Macmillan's abortive attempt to enter the EEC in the early 1960s.

3 The Pay Board produced a report in the middle of the election campaign which seemed to show that the Coal Board had got its sums wrong, and that the miners could have been given more money without breaching Phase 3. If this was true, the whole confrontation had been unnecessary.

4 For a very interesting account of this strange episode in our recent history, see *The Fall of Heath* by Stephen Fay and Hugo Young, published by the *Sunday Times*.

5 For a fuller analysis, see Appendix 6.

6 These were: motor manufacture, mechanical engineering, electrical engineering, food

manufacturing, foundries, paper and board, machine tools, electronics, chemicals, textiles, clothing.

7 Labour won 301 seats out of 625; the Conservatives had 296. Of the other parties, the Liberals had 14, the United Ulster Unionists, who had broken away from the Conservatives, had 11, the Scottish and Welsh Nationalists combined had 9, others 4. The emergence of regional parties in Scotland, Wales and Northern Ireland was a new and ominous feature, which was to become even more marked in the October 1974 election. In the case of Scotland particularly, dissatisfaction with the UK's poor economic performance was a significant factor in this rise.

8 Governments in the 1960s had been much influenced by the Paish theory, that the economy was best run with a margin of spare capacity; and by the Phillips curve, which indicated that there was a trade-off between unemployment and wage inflation—the higher the unemployment, the lower the wage pressure. Neither theory stood up well to the actual circumstances encountered after 1968. Clearly union bargaining power was such that big wage increases could still be won in conditions of substantial unemployment—though the recession of the mid-1970s was to provide some tantalisingly tentative evidence that *very* high unemployment might have *some* restraining effect on wage demands after all.

9 There was an interregnum period of some months between Sir Frank's departure and Sir Ronald's arrival, during which T C Fraser served as acting director-general of NEDO.

10 In fact, at a crucial stage, responsibility for drafting the Bill was taken out of the hands of the Department of Industry and transferred to the Cabinet Office, under the personal supervision of the Prime Minister. There is little doubt that this was partly the result of discreet backstairs pressure by the CBI. The net effect was in the end to remove from the Bill the element of industrial democracy, so that planning agreements became not only optional, but bilateral rather than trilateral in nature.

11 As I did, in *The Stagnant Society* (Penguin, Harmondsworth, 1961 and 1972).

12 One of the Conservative innovations retained by Labour was the hiving-off of the Department of Employment's responsibilities in the field of manpower planning, training, re-training and job creation to a new public agency, the Manpower Services Commission (MSC). The MSC was given the task of developing the kind of positive manpower policies which had been developed over the years most effectively in Sweden and West Germany. There is little doubt that in future it will play a bigger role than heretofore in industrial strategy work at micro level. Like NEDC, the MSC is run on a tripartite basis by government, CBI and TUC.

13 The government was much influenced in its thinking by the 'structural' analysis of Britain's economic problem set out in *Britain's Economic Problem: Too Few Producers* by Robert Bacon and Walter Eltis (Macmillan, London, 1976), which is discussed further in Chapter 5.

14 These were: iron and steel, organic chemicals, pharmaceuticals, plastics, synthetic rubber, ferrous foundries, non-ferrous foundries, machine tools, pumps and valves, process plant fabrications, fluid power equipment, industrial engines, textile machinery, construction equipment, mechanical handling equipment, industrial trucks, office machinery, mining machinery, printing machinery, heating ventilating and air conditioning equipment, constructional steelwork, drop forgings, machinery for food and drink processing packing and bottling, automation and instrumentation, electronic components, computers, heavy electrical machinery, industrial equipment, domestic electrical appliances, radio radar and electronic capital goods, man-made fibres, wool textiles, knitwear, clothing, food and drink, paper and board, rubber processing, bearings, gears. There were some notable omissions, such as the motor industry and the nationalised industries other than steel.

15 One of the problems encountered by some of the EDCs, such as mechanical engineering, was that they covered so wide a field that it was difficult to establish any organic unity. The breakdown into sectors with more clearly defined frontiers and common characteristics and interests made for more meaningful discussion. Of the sectors, no fewer than seventeen were within the territory encompassed by the mechanical engineering EDC.

16 The precise formula was that wage increases had to be negotiated with an individual
weekly limit of £2.50 or 5% of total earnings, whichever was greater, subject to a
maximum of £4. The twelve-month interval between major pay increases would
continue to apply.

17 Sir Eric Roll had been the first permanent secretary of the DEA, and was now chairman
of a merchant bank and an independent member of the NEDC.

18 Relations between industry and the City had troubled NEDC for some time. Attempts to
establish a City EDC going back over ten years had been blocked by the Bank of
England. There were periodic complaints that the City was not providing the financial
support for British industry that it should—that it was lending abroad while British
industry went short of funds (though nobody disputed that overseas investment produced a better return). It was also argued that because of its dependence on equity
capital as opposed to fixed-interest borrowing, British industry had low gearing and was
thus precluded from expanding as fast as, say, Japanese businesses where the equity
base was low, but where government provided a protection against the vulnerability to
takeovers which would' normally result from very high gearing.

The Roll working party was set up in 1975 to investigate this whole rather murky
area. Its remit was to establish whether or not the supply of funds was a serious constraint on the performance of manufacturing industry, and whether it was likely to be so
during the expected upswing of 1976-8. In the course of this work it was planning to
produce a model of the source and application of funds for the economy as a whole.
The working group also had under examination the scope for counter-cyclical or other
investment schemes which government might introduce, and an inventory of other ideas
for possible reform of the UK financial system.

19 The strategy was in fact to be put to the test unexpectedly soon. During the autumn
further turbulence in the international money market led to renewed pressure on sterling, whose exchange rate fell sharply, to a point at which speculation became intense.
The old problem of the sterling balances returned, as the OPEC creditors who had been
encouraged to bank their surpluses in Britain began to withdraw their money in view of
its continued depreciation. Once again the government had to take immediate action to
stem the drain on the reserves. Interest rates were pushed up to unprecedentedly high
levels, sharp reductions imposed on public spending, and a massive new loan negotiated
with the International Monetary Fund (IMF). These policies imposed severe strains on
the internal cohesion of the Labour movement, and on the confidence of industry—
especially as they coincided with indications that the world recovery from recession was
faltering, and that a further rise in oil prices was in prospect. The debut of the 1976
industrial strategy was thus an unhappy one. While the government reiterated its
determination to implement the strategy, and to give priority to industrial investment,
there was little evidence at the end of the year that industry believed the times—and the
cost of money—were propitious for a new round of investment. Despite its declared
intention to help industry, the government had in fact added a new incubus to industry's
costs by increasing employers' National Insurance contributions. Britain's basic problems showed no sign of immediate resolution. And, with unemployment at crisis levels
and showing no sign of falling, the social contract was under increasing strain. There
was general agreement that a further period of income restraint would be necessary
when the existing agreement lapsed in July 1977, but growing doubt as to whether it
would be possible to negotiate an agreement which would inevitably have to involve a
further reduction in real incomes—given that inflation was still running at around
14-15%, and looked like continuing to do so (especially if the exchange rate of the
pound went on falling). The question of the government's ability to control events in
any form was being posed more and more sharply as 1976 drew to its unhappy close.

# 5 Planning: Lessons, Issues and Options

It will hardly have escaped notice that the period covered in the previous four chapters has seen the sharpest decline in Britain's relative economic strength and wealth of any in recent history. On this basis one could hardly call national planning a success so far. Was this the fault of the plans themselves? Of the environment in which they were made? Is the whole exercise of national economic planning mistaken or counter-productive?

## DO WE NEED A PLAN?

The last question is the one which must be dealt with first, though I believe it can be answered relatively briefly. Any plan worthy of the name, whether it be by a government, a business enterprise, or whatever, must contain two elements—a *forecast* and a *strategy*. The forecast seeks to identify what is likely to happen, so that threats can be identified and warded off, opportunities prepared for and seized. Few people today are prepared to argue that forecasting *per se* is wrong or impossible, and few would argue that a genuine exchange of views about the future is useless. Indeed, whether it wishes to or not, government today has to forecast future trends in some detail in order to plan its own public expenditure, including investment by the nationalised industries.

The strategy seeks to establish agreed objectives for the organisation doing the planning, and to assure the means for the achievement of these ends; almost invariably, this involves a choice between conflicting object-ives, and measures to deploy resources in such a way as to secure the preferred objective, at the expense of the others. Is it sensible for a government to seek to do this, either by itself or in partnership with other entities within the body politic—or can it leave the whole question of the allocation of resources to market forces?

The relationship between the market economy and strategic planning is a complex one. On the one hand it is plainly perverse to ignore or seek to work against market forces in determining one's strategy—particularly if one is operating in an open economy like the UK, with a high degree of dependence on world trade. There is no necessary conflict between planning and the market economy, if by 'planning' one means the kinds of exercises described in this book. On the other hand it is difficult to abdicate from the responsibility of seeking to steer the allocation of resources, in response to or in anticipation of market forces, in the circumstances of a complex modern economy like Britain's: an economy where the public sector accounts for over half the total GNP, and where there is a very high degree of interdependence between the different sectors of the economy.

Of course, a strategy does not need to be buttressed by an elaborate structure of quantitative forecasts. It is a fair criticism of most of the planning exercises described in the preceding chapters that the forecasting element tended to submerge the strategic highlights (sometimes, as in the National Plan, deliberately)—and much of the forecasting was, as we have seen, suspect. It is perfectly feasible, as the Roy Jenkins chancellorship shows, to operate a clearly defined (if in some respects inadequate) strategy without any under-pinning of planning for the private sector. But the limitations of that strategy in the event suggest that things might have gone better had there been a 'micro' element to complement the (for the postwar era, exceptionally clear and single-minded) 'macro' strategy.

Plainly, a national strategy has to be realistic and attainable. It must therefore be based on facts. But how is one to ensure that realism is attained? How are the planners—whether in government or outside—to see that the strategy is understood, accepted and implemented? In the implementation, how far is it wise or legitimate to try to 'bend' market forces by the use of special incentives, legislation or controls? These, it seems to me, are the important questions to ask, rather than the arid or rhetorical question: 'To plan or not to plan?'

Clearly in this respect a national plan is in a different category from corporate plans. In the latter case all the resources of the unit being planned are under the control of those approving the plan. In a national plan the government or planning agency only has direct control over those resources in the public sector. So, as regards the private sector, national plans can range through a whole spectrum from the purely indicative (in which case the strategic element is muted) through the normative (like the original Neddy Plan) to varying degrees of the coercive. It is the coercive element that most people find offensive in national planning. But that element has been almost totally lacking in British economic planning over the past fifteen years. Of course there have been various attempts—some sensible, some misjudged, some linked with a planning exercise, some not—to influence the allocation of resources by special incentives or disincentives. But I am not aware of any significant school of thought in any country today which denies *in principle* the wisdom or admissibility of governments seeking to influence or correct market forces by such actions. The argument is over the objectives and the measures chosen, rather than whether there should be any.

One can make many technical criticisms of the quality of the various planning documents. Nearly all of them were overoptimistic on the balance of payments. In the earlier plans the dialogue with industry was, inevitably, rushed and therefore superficial, and assumptions were made on very flimsy evidence. In the early plans, too, there was an attempt to reach spurious consistency when what the planners should have been doing was probing inconsistencies in order to expose problems and pose options. There was a kind of underlying belief that growth could be achieved if you simply talked about it long enough.

DO WE NEED A STRATEGY?

But the real fundamental criticism that has to be made is that at no time up to 1976—with the partial exception, as indicated above, of the Jenkins chancellorship—did the government have an overall economic strategy to which its various individual policies were related, which persisted over any length of time.

One is forced to the conclusion that for most of the time governments have played at planning, while the real business of policy making has been a matter of improvisation, reaction to outside pressures, and short-term expediency. Let us take a few examples. The original Neddy Plan and *The Task Ahead* were abandoned because there was a change of government, the National Plan and the 1972 Industrial Review because short-term changes in the external environment appeared to invalidate some of the basic assumptions. This readiness to abandon plans rather than to re-work and modify them is symptomatic. The French and the Japanese, by contrast, have been prepared to modify and adjust plans to a considerable degree when it seems necessary. One cannot help feeling that the reason is that for them the plan is important as a basis for national strategic decision, rather than a prestige gimmick to be hurriedly discarded if it does not receive instant acclaim, or if circumstances change.

Most people today accept that one element in a successful strategy for economic advance in Britain must be a policy of income restraint. Yet at no time until 1976 was the linkage successfully established in economic policy making between incomes restraint in the short term and economic growth in the longer term. Governments imposed statutory incomes policies when forced into a balance-of-payments crisis. Incomes policies were not normally seen as alternatives to deflation, but as accompaniments to it: 'freeze' came with 'squeeze', rather than instead of it. In such circumstances it was exceptionally difficult to convince trade unionists that long-term income restraint, or the planned growth of incomes, was a positive and necessary element in a long-term growth strategy, rather than a piece of temporary governmental brutality to be got rid of as soon as possible.

In other words, Britain has been consistently bad since the war at making strategic choices, at relating the different strands of policy to a coherent whole. For part of the explanation one must look to the civil service, for part to the two-party political system, for part to the self-balancing nature of our institutional and social structure, which makes radical change peculiarly difficult to achieve.

Let us look first at the role of Whitehall—which means, in this context, essentially the Treasury. The attitude of the Treasury towards Neddy has tended to be one of scepticism and cynicism—as it was, but to a much stronger degree, towards the DEA. None of the plans produced by DEA or NEDC up to the 1976 industrial strategy have been accepted as control documents for government economic policy (with the possible exception of the Maudling 'dash for growth' period, and even here the Chancellor's decision to boost consumer spending ran counter to NEDC advice). Moreover, there has been a continuing problem about the provision of Treasury forecasts for Neddy.

Since the beginning of the 1960s, the Treasury has been responsible for preparing a regular medium-term economic forecast which has been used as the basis for macro-economic policy and specifically for the programming and control of public spending; public spending programmes are rolled forward annually to a five-year horizon. This exercise is conducted in conditions of considerable secrecy. The published versions of the public expenditure programme conceal most of the critical assumptions behind the government's thinking, and the medium-term economic forecast itself is never published. The public spending programme is not normally discussed in the NEDC.

There are of course good reasons for the government's caution. The revelation of what the Treasury really thinks is going to happen to the domestic inflation rate or the exchange rate for sterling, say, could be embarrassing politically. Moreover, the evidence suggests that the medium-term forecast has not been notably more accurate than the NEDC's. Nevertheless, one is left with the impression that a dual system of planning has been in operation in postwar Britain. There is the 'public' system exemplified in the Neddy structure, and the covert system practised by government using Treasury forecasts which are not revealed, based on thinking which is also kept secret; and there is no guarantee that the two systems are working on the same assumptions or the same figures.

The secretive attitude of the Treasury has been a characteristic of the British government system since the war. It is perhaps not without significance that the three NEDC planning initiatives taken since the demise of the National Plan were all launched after prodding by the CBI and TUC, who wanted a way of opening up the debate on economic strategy and probing the government's own thinking.

Tension between NEDC and government is inevitable, and in a sense that was what the NEDC was set up to provide. Whether that tension is creative or otherwise depends very largely on the chairman of NEDC, who except during the lifetime of the DEA has always been the Prime Minister or Chancellor. And it may be that the problem of separate and possibly conflicting forecasts is becoming less serious as the UK economy becomes increasingly open to external economic influences, and as British industry increasingly sees its relevant market as a world and not a national one. (The problem of adjusting planning systems designed for a largely closed economy to the new uncertainties and priorities caused by the opening up of trading opportunities can be serious, as the changes between the first three French national plans and the second three, which followed the setting-up of the European Common Market, show.)

At the same time, one is forced to the conclusion that no British Government has yet fully thought through the implications of national planning, either institutionally or on the process of decision making. What should be an integrated strategy is still being evolved in patchwork fashion, worked on by different groups of people at different times and places, in the hope that somehow the whole when it emerges will magically cohere.

PARLIAMENT AND THE CORPORATE STATE

Nowhere is this more true than in the relations with Parliament. The problem of reconciling consensus planning with a two-party democracy based on adversary politics is plainly an intractable one. It is no coincidence that the two Western-style democracies which have been most successful in evolving and operating national planning systems aimed at economic growth have been Japan and France. In Japan the Liberal Democratic Party has been in power continuously since the war. In France under the Fourth Republic parliamentary instability was such that no elected government exercised effective power, and the country was in practice governed by the civil service; the Fifth Republic has so far seen a continuation of Gaullist or Conservative administrations, with a weak and hitherto divided parliamentary opposition. In both these cases therefore it has been possible to ensure a high degree of continuity in economic policy.

To some extent the same has been true of countries which operate systems of proportional representation, such as West Germany or the Benelux countries. In these cases the ability of any new government to move too far away from the policies of its predecessor is limited, because any government is likely to be a coalition; this means that the scope for political U-turns or bold new initiatives is circumscribed, and businessmen can bank on a reasonable degree of continuity in government policy. This is an enormous benefit to business enterprises planning long-term investments and market strategies.

By contrast, in the UK it is precisely this element of continuity—which must be at the base of any credible system of national planning—which has been missing. Since Britain's basic political problem is perceived as being economic weakness, the parliamentary opposition is always under pressure to distance itself from the government's economic policy and develop its own alternative strategy which can be put to the voters. Thus every new government brings in new policies, which usually have to be altered after two years (Labour in 1966 and again in 1975, the Conservatives in 1972), when they are seen to be irrelevant to the problems actually facing the country: problems of which no opposition party can hope to be fully informed. The situation is worsened by the fact that our two main political parties tend to identify, in opposition especially, with capital and labour respectively; thus not only their ideas but their values tend to differ.

This makes for exciting politics, but for low-credibility government strategies, whichever party is in power. The businessman listens to what the government tells him with a sceptical ear, knowing that the spin of the parliamentary wheel is likely to make today's panacea tomorrow's anathema, and in these circumstances the course of prudence is to make the fewest possible commitments and play safe. And thus despite all the exhortations and very real incentives provided by successive governments, Britain has become an increasingly under-capitalised economy.

How in these circumstances is planning to acquire the assurance of continuity which it needs to carry credibility? Radical ideas, like giving the main opposition party representation on the NEDC, tend to be rejected with varying degrees of scorn or reluctance. There may be more hope for a modified version of this proposal, namely, that the non-government members of NEDC should hold regular meetings with the Opposition leaders. But the possibility of taking economic planning right out of party politics seems remote, however desirable.

There may be more scope for involving Parliament in the planning process by submitting to it all major agreed NEDC reports,[1] and establishing a Parliamentary Select Committee to keep Neddy and all its works under regular review. This idea has fairly widespread support among NEDC members, both ministers and others, and has been publicly canvassed by Lord Watkinson, a former Conservative Cabinet minister who became president of the CBI in 1976.

This involvement of Parliament might not only help eventually to create the possibility of a bipartisan policy on planning and economic strategy. It might also avert the risk of a parliamentary backlash against what is seen as 'the creeping corporate state'.[2] As more and more decisions in the economic field are seen as being taken in the NEDC or other tripartite bodies, outside Parliament, the question of ultimate democratic authority is likely to be posed. Inept though Parliament is in dealing with industrial matters, or issues involving management and workers, it is still the sovereign elected body in the land, whereas NEDC members are appointed, not elected. So by some means or other Parliament needs to be involved in the process of decision making on economic strategy.

THE IMPORTANCE OF TRIPARTISM

In fact one of the persistent questions surrounding the whole Neddy structure is the precise contribution and status of the different partners.

The decision to establish a tripartite body alongside but outside government, and to give it specific responsibility for national planning, taken apparently lightheartedly fifteen years ago, was in fact a very far-reaching one. No other major Western country has used exactly the same formula. Other countries have national plans—but they are normally prepared inside government, and do not involve the trade unions (the French and Japanese planning dialogues are essentially bipartite, between government and industry, not tripartite; this reflects the weakness of the trade union movement in both countries). This inevitably simplifies discussion.

Other countries, again, have tripartite advisory bodies of great authority operating alongside government; one might mention in this context the Benelux countries, the Scandinavians or Austria. These bodies typically discuss the broad guidelines of national economic, industrial and social strategy, and they may supervise incomes policies. But they do not formulate national plans in the Neddy sense. Only in the UK have the two functions been combined.

Even in the UK, of course, the situation is not entirely clear-cut. Only at exceptional times has the NEDC itself been used as a bargaining forum to determine the details of prices and incomes policy, and then unsuccessfully. But since the bargainers are in most cases the same people who meet around the Neddy table, the separation of functions between planning and wage bargaining is often more apparent than real—and a great deal of the NEDC's work, such as the regular debates on growth, profits, productivity and export competitiveness, bear directly on prices and incomes policy. Also, in recent years some of the key discussions on social policy which in other countries have been handled by tripartite Economic and Social Committees, in the UK have been dealt with bilaterally in the context of the social contract between the Labour Government and the TUC. But one imagines that in due course these discussions too will become to some extent trilateral.

Neither the TUC nor the CBI members of the NEDC or the EDCs can enter into commitments as can the government representatives, nor can they speak with the same degree of authority. This was very evident in the early stages, when commitments by employer organisations and the TUC to voluntary price and wage restraint had little or no effect on the behaviour of their members.

Nevertheless, during the 1970s the ability of the central organisations to commit their members has demonstrably grown; witness the CBI price restraint in 1971-2, and the TUC wage restraint in 1975-6. In other areas, of course, their authority is more limited. CBI pressure on members to step up investment, or TUC pressure to end shopfloor restrictive practices, are unlikely *per se* to get much response. The power is limited, but it is there. And the more it is seen to exist, the more uneasy Parliament is likely to become.[3]

So the tripartite consensus is a reality, with all its evident limitations.[4] If economic planning is to be meaningful, it is sensible for it to carry the approval of the NEDC. Even the National Plan did that.

The detailed preparation of plans has to be the joint responsibility of government departments and NEDO, and the final result has to be seen to be reflected in government policy making. The evidence is that Whitehall has found the feed-in of information from the EDCs and sector working groups more useful in many ways than any of the other channels through which the private sector has communicated with government. And this is of vital importance, for one of the weaknesses of British economic management in the past (by contrast with France or Japan, for example) has been poor communication between Whitehall and industry.[5]

CRITICS OF TRIPARTISM

'Tripartism' or 'consensus planning' has its critics, to left and right in the political spectrum. The right-wing view is that government should deal at arm's length with capital and labour; that it should not seek to intervene in industry beyond the absolute minimum; that it should try to cut state spending and reduce its commitments; that it should control the economy by regulating overall demand and in particular by paying more attention to the money supply than in the past; that it should not try to control wages or prices. It is unlikely that this policy, if applied again, would be any more successful than it was in 1970 (though it is true that in 1970-4 the government did not control the money supply at all effectively). And, while most businessmen warm to it instinctively, the CBI leadership would almost certainly privately advise against it. A future Conservative Government, whatever its inclinations, would in practice have to come to terms with the planning structure more or less as it exists today.

Perhaps a more serious challenge, though one which is currently in retreat, is that posed by the Left, whose most articulate spokesman has been Mr Wedgwood Benn. The thesis of the Left has been that the corporate state as represented in the Neddy structure is not only undemocratic, but inefficient; because its leaders cannot in practice commit their constituents except to a very limited degree. Thus, for example, an EDC or a sector working party might make sense in a few industries where there are small firms and reasonably strong trade associations; but over much of the economy this situation simply does not apply. If one wants action, therefore, in most cases one has to go direct to the individual firms. Hence the importance of planning agreements, and of agencies like the IRC and NEB which can directly influence the decisions of boards of directors by applying financial aid or pressure.

If this were the whole of the message, it would find a reasonable measure of agreement. Planning agreements as an adjunct to national and sector planning are now generally accepted. Nearly everybody agrees that closer contacts between large firms and the government are desirable in modern conditions, if only as part of a necessary process of mutual education. Many of those who have participated in the work of NEDC and the EDCs are strongly critical of the lack of follow-up, of the difficulty of making such bodies 'action-oriented'. It is significant that NEDC's minutes are never 'actioned', unlike the check-lists for action in the National Plan and the industrial strategy reports. During the 1960s some of the EDCs presented excellent reports indicating the need for urgent action—the report produced by the process plant working party is a good example—which were simply not followed up because the different firms in the industry could not accept the need for action or could not agree among themselves on a solution.

But the 'alternative strategy' of the Left goes beyond this. First, it puts a high value on state intervention as against consensus planning. Again, most people today would accept that direct intervention has a role to play in the evolution of a national strategy, though they would differ profoundly on how large or small a role it should be—and in their degree of scepticism about the ability of any government or public agency to invest its (or rather our, the taxpayers') money wisely in commercial ventures.

The Left, however, argues that there has been a profound shift in the nature of our society in recent years, and that power effectively now resides, not only in the boardroom, but on the shopfloor. The shop stewards' committee is as important as the board of directors. This trend should be encouraged because it is only by getting the commitment of the workers directly that one can make the productivity breakthrough on which our future depends. Thus industrial democracy should be stimulated, not only by putting worker representatives on the board of directors as in Germany, Sweden or the Netherlands, but by giving the worker more autonomy in determining his work pattern, and by encouraging worker co-operatives and moves towards worker control on the Yugoslav pattern.

## POPULISM IS NOT ENOUGH!

From the political point of view, this approach is of course profoundly subversive, not only as regards the CBI—who vehemently opposed planning agreements so long as Wedgwood Benn was the minister responsible for them, seeing them as an overt step towards worker control; but also as regards the TUC. For the direct appeal to the workers is being made in a sense over the heads of their elected leaders, the national officials of the unions. For some years at the end of the 1960s and the beginning of the 1970s the leaders of the two biggest trade unions, the transport workers and the engineers, encouraged the decentralisation of decision making in an attempt to make their unions more democratic in the Benn sense—that is, more populist, less élitist. But the pressures of the mid-1970s have forced a partial abandonment of this policy, and a reinforcement of centralist leadership on the Swedish or German model; and thus the union leaders have moved away from the Left on this as on other issues.

During 1974 and early 1975, when the populist, interventionist policy of Wedgwood Benn was given free rein, the involvement of workers in the decision-making process tended to mean that a high premium was put on using public money to maintain jobs, often in very unsuitable industries; and a low priority on encouraging mobility and efficiency. Critics would say that this is an inevitable effect. If you decide that you want to involve the workers' representatives in decision making, in order to tap the unused enthusiasm and expertise bottled up by a class-dominated social structure, clearly you have to put a high premium on the advice they give; for if you ask for it and then disregard it, you risk worsening the alienation and cynicism you are trying to dissipate. But the concern of the workers' representatives at local level is primarily with the preservation of local jobs; they are not interested professionally in the broader requirements of the national economy; that is not their function. And so the attempt to broaden the basis of decision making by appealing to the masses directly rather than via their elected representatives can lead to an abdication of responsibility. This is the classic dilemma of direct as against representative democracy.

Since 1975 the attempt to substitute a populist approach to our problems for Neddy-type consensus planning has been in partial eclipse. The short-term costs at a time of economic crisis were too obvious. Too many top people in too many power centres felt themselves threatened by it. The country was not ready for the kind of revolution implied.

But the problem remains, even if Benn-type populism is not (as I believe it is not) the solution. Despite all the efforts, the consensus arrived at around the Neddy top table *is* a consensus of élites. The nation has never felt itself passionately involved in the issues or in their solutions. Communication has always been the planners' greatest problem, and it remains so. One of the difficulties about planning agreements from the TUC's point of view is the weakness of plant bargaining machinery at the official union level, so that if these agreements had developed as Wedgwood Benn intended, control on the union side would have passed in many cases away from the union hierarchy into the hands of shop stewards. On the CBI side, too, communication up and down the line remains a major weakness—especially at the EDC level, where the CBI has never been officially represented. So, if the 1976 industrial strategy is seen to fail as the previous planning exercises have failed, there is a strong likelihood that the mood of the country will start to polarise around the two visible alternatives—the 'stand-back' attitude of the Right, and the heady populism of the Left. The debate is by no means over.

Nor is it a trivial issue. All the evidence suggests that those who have been privileged to participate in the national debate as members of the NEDC or the more successful EDCs have found it an educational experience. Years of discussion have visibly moulded the attitudes of the participants. The TUC leaders, for example, clearly see the role of business profits in much more constructive and less emotive terms than in the past. The CBI participants, too, have become notably more tolerant of the problems faced by ministers and union leaders.

PRODUCTIVITY AND INDUSTRIAL STRUCTURE

All this is to the good. Yet ministers who were on the NEDC in the 1960s and returned to it after the 1974 election report that they were struck by the similarity of the discussions there. NEDC was still discussing the same issues, the same problems; the debate on industrial efficiency in the 1976 industrial strategy exercise was still churning over the same ground as that covered in the debates on the Orange Book and the National Plan. The gramophone needle seems to have got stuck in the same groove.

That groove is the persistently low productivity of much (not all) of British industry. In May 1976 the NEDO published a very important monograph comparing the performance sector-by-sector of UK and West German manufacturing industry from 1954 to 1972. The message was the same as that which EDC after EDC has hammered home year after year. Across almost the whole field of manufacturing industry, German firms on average use their assets better than all but the best British firms. The structure of manufacturing in the two countries is broadly comparable—and so is the performance of the best firms in the two countries. But in most industries the variation in performance between the best and the worst firms has been far more marked in the UK than in Germany. This is what has pulled down our national economic performance in good years and bad alike, and has rendered us weak and vulnerable.

So any strategy to improve the national economy must focus on the productivity issue, on ways of improving the supply side of the economy as well as the demand side. This is partly a matter of developing counter-cyclical measures to ensure better use of assets over the cycle (to avoid bunching of demand for capital goods at the peak, when prices are high and delivery dates extended); partly a question of attacking sector by sector the particular identifiable constraints to growth and efficiency, as the sector working parties set up in 1975 aimed to do; and partly—and this where the mainspring is still missing—enthusing people at all levels in industry to give of their best, and to accept and promote radical changes in our social and institutional structure, to give a higher value to growth and efficiency and a lower value to security and status. Britain is like a pendulum which oscillates violently from side to side, but always comes back to rest in the same spot. The vibrations are tremendous, but the balance of forces seems to ensure that nothing actually changes. This is what we have to alter, but the way of doing it has so far eluded all our postwar leaders.

What is it that planning ought to have done which it has not done? If we had had a real national strategy over the last decade and a half, one point on which it would surely have focused would have been the national allocation of resources between the different main outlets—

investment, exports, consumer spending, public expenditure; and between those outputs which are traded in the market and those which are not. We have seen that in a rather general way governments tried to give priority to exports and investment in their various attempts at planning. But we have also seen that other factors (short-term efforts to boost the economy, electoral pressures, reluctance to devalue, etc.) tended to get in the way of these objectives.

Early in 1976 a very influential analysis, *Britain's Economic Problem: Too Few Producers*, by Robert Bacon and Walter Eltis (published by Macmillan), sought to explain Britain's poor performance over this period by analysing the changing structure of the economy. Bacon and Eltis pointed out that in the decade 1965-75 the rate of growth of industrial production had halved by comparison with the previous decade (17% against 35%); inflation had risen from 3.1% a year in 1955-65 to 7% in 1965-74, and 26% in 1974-5 (it is fair to say that it receded again in 1975-6); unemployment rose from 1.9% in the first decade to 2.7% in the second, and 5% in 1975. The pound's exchange rate compared to other main currencies rose slightly in 1955-65, but dropped by 38% in the subsequent decade. The incidence of strikes also worsened substantially over the same period (though again there was a big improvement in 1975-6).

At the same time, despite our poor productivity relative to our main competitors, absolute productivity has improved substantially in manufacturing industry. We saw earlier that productivity in British industry at the time of the National Plan was growing at just over 3% a year. Ten years later it was growing at more than 4% a year—faster in fact than the growth in national product; so what was happening to the resources released by the higher productivity?

The answer, according to Bacon and Eltis, is the key to Britain's economic problem. Numbers employed in manufacturing industry dropped by 14% between 1965 and 1975, despite a substantial fall in hours worked. Some of this drop was represented by a higher level of unemployment, but more important was the marked shift of manpower out of industry into service trades, and particularly into the public sector. Employment outside industry relative to industrial employment grew by one-third between 1961 and 1974. The extra wealth created by industry has been syphoned off, as it were, into the non-market sector of public services, to a degree which has happened in no other country, and this lies at the root of our failure over the last decade. The extra resources channelled into the non-market public sector have had to be paid for out of the dwindling profits of the productive sector, with the result that there has been no margin left to sustain the investment programme needed to keep industry efficient and competitive.

Non-market (predominantly state) expenditure as a proportion of the total rose from around 40% to around 60% between 1961 and 1974. (These figures included transfer payments and some public sector industry spending, and have been subject to some revision since Bacon and Eltis wrote their book.) Not only did this erode profits and pre-empt resources which could have been better used in the productive sector; it also stimulated wage inflation, by creating new demands for labour and adding to the tax burden on incomes. Thus the growth potential correctly identified in the Neddy and National Plans has been frittered away through a misallocation of resources by successive governments.[6]

Such, in essence, is the 'structuralist' argument—and, despite its oversimplifications, it clearly has force. Over the period in question successive British governments, for what seemed at the time to be cogent short-term reasons, took decisions affecting the allocation of national resources which in no way conformed to a reasonable long-term strategy or to the priorities which they themselves professed. Such behaviour, continued over a period of years, is the negation of planning.

The Labour Government in 1976 seemed to have taken the message. The government's strategy, as expressed by both Prime Minister Callaghan and his Chancellor Denis Healey, has been to leave room in the economic upswing for resources to move to industrial investment, by cutting public spending and holding back private consumption by reducing real incomes through the counter-inflation policy; exports should grow anyway as world economic activity rises, so long as sterling continues to float and the rise in domestic spending is kept down. The intentions are good, but it remains to be seen whether they can be translated into effective action.

THE SOCIAL DIMENSION

At the same time, it is clear that the world is becoming a much more complex place, and one of the major new areas of complexity is the inter-relation between economic and social policy. This relationship is many-faceted. If the relatively simple demand-and-supply relationships established by Keynes no longer apply—so that wages and unemployment increase together, or taxes designed to take money out of circulation instead fuel inflation further by stimulating wage demands—it is not because the economic equations themselves are wrong, but because new social and institutional factors have started to intrude. The wage explosion at the end of the 1960s reflected new social pressures and institutional strengths rather than high labour demand. Similarly, social pressures in recent years have reduced labour mobility by increasing job security and have significantly modified the pattern of rewards in society.

Moreover, the social expenditures of government have themselves become, as we have just seen, a major element in the economy. And if, as seems clear, some form of income restraint has to be a part of national strategy for growth or even survival, it can only operate as part of an overall social contract which will embrace other factors, such as the 'social wage', the division of the national wealth, the broad thrust of government social policy and spending, and the extension of non-wage benefits such as participation in industrial management, job security, job enrichment and industrial democracy.

The area of economic planning, in other words, has to be extended to include at least some element of social planning as well. For it is in their misjudgement of the social element that economic plans in modern democracies only too often fail.

Discussion of the social dimension in economic planning has made little headway so far in the UK, and considering the heavy weather we have made of the limited kind of planning we have undertaken so far, one hesitates to recommend adding another area of complexity to an already complicated picture. But I believe, for the reasons given above, that we are more likely in the long run to make a success of our economic strategy if we take the social dimension seriously than if we continue to try to ignore it.

In fact, during 1975 and 1976 government has begun to give some thought to this—partly because of the need to establish priorities in its own social spending at a time of real reduction in resources, due to the combination of curtailed spending and sharply rising costs. The Central Policy Review Staff (the so-called Cabinet Office 'think-tank') has undertaken a number of studies, both across-the-board and in particular policy areas, to illuminate some of the major problems, and to try to establish a basis for a much more systematic evaluation of the major options open in the social field. But it will be some time before government, or for that matter the CBI or TUC, will be ready for the kind of public discussion on social policy priorities which occurs, for example, in Sweden and Austria—a discussion in which options are quantified and analysed in a non-political and objective manner.

Nevertheless, I believe this will be the next major challenge for Neddy, if and when the 1975-6 industrial strategy exercise, both in its short-term and medium-term dimension, is seen to have succeeded. The day when the Council can debate the major social options as lucidly as it can discuss, say, ways and means of stimulating investment, will be the day it has really come of age.

THE FRENCH CONNECTION

This is one area where French planning may have lessons for us in the late 1970s, as it did in the early 1960s. French planning has evolved considerably since the days when it seemed to offer Britain a way out of stagnation and 'stop-go'. The first three French plans (1947-61) were concerned essentially with the reconstruction of the country's economy after the war, and so with the allocation of investment to priority sectors and providing a growth environment for private industry. Since the economy was still relatively self-contained, *dirigiste* policies could be used fairly freely to enforce the plans.

The situtation changed when France entered the European Common Market and had to compete directly with Germany and the other EEC countries. The main theme of the fourth, fifth and sixth plans (1962-75) was making French industry more competitive. Their impact on national life was much less than that of the first two plans. As the economy became more open, so the plan became less normative and more indicative. But the government's ability and willingness to use the selective credit weapon to steer industry in directions indicated by the planners remains.

All French plans since the fourth have been formally submitted to and discussed in Parliament, and this has given them an increasing political and social orientation. This is particularly marked in the Seventh Plan (1976-80), which is deliberately aimed at establishing a consensus to meet the social challenges facing France. The three main objectives of the Seventh Plan are to restore the French balance of payments by 1980, to maintain full employment and to control inflation. These are seen as the necessary conditions for four social goals:

(1) To provide the economic conditions necessary for full employment and social progress covering demographic growth and control, modernisation of the educational system and development of a modern competitive and balanced industry.
(2) To raise the quality of life including the improvement of employment conditions and the status of manual work; a new family policy; improvement of housing and town planning; curtailing excessive growth of big cities and control of environmental pollution.
(3) To reduce inequalities, particularly of incomes, and to improve the access of all to public services.
(4) To achieve a higher degree of devolution of decision making at the regional level.

Clearly, the French Seventh Plan covers a wider canvas than any of the UK planning initiatives, not excluding the 1965 National Plan. It articulates, in fact, a quantified vision of society, a set of objectives which are intended to delineate the strategy to be followed by the French Government and public authorities to 1980. It is precisely this comprehensive vision that British governments, it seems to me, have been lacking.

This is not to say, of course, that such broad social issues and objectives are absent from the British political dialogue. They are set out, often in considerable detail, in party manifestos and policy documents of one kind or another—including, since 1974, the social contract. But what has been missing, at least to my mind, in the British political dialogue is any clear integration of the social and economic objectives, any clear analysis of the strategic options facing the nation or of the trade-offs which are possible and desirable as between economic and social ends.

It is also true that there are special elements in the French scene which are missing in this country, which would make a straightforward transplantation of the French system in its entirety impracticable. Among the Western democracies, France has been peculiarly backward in the development of its social system. It has remained a country of glaring social inequality. It is also the one country in the EEC whose political system has had to cope with a quasi-revolutionary situation not once but twice since the war: first in 1957, when the Fourth Republic was overturned in what amounted to a bloodless *coup d'état* by the Gaullist Fifth Republic; and again in 1968, when student unrest coincided with a general strike which nearly brought down the Gaullist regime.

These events have made modern French governments very sensitive to the need for social reform, while the country's social and political structure—a weak and fragmented labour movement, a dominant right-wing parliamentary majority, the dominance of the Left over much of the postwar era by a Communist Party which has been outside the political dialogue—have made such reform peculiarly difficult to achieve. In other words, France has been a country where the signals of left-wing protest are for a democracy peculiarly muted, due to the weakness of the unions and parliamentary opposition, with the result that when protest comes it may come with explosive suddenness. The missing element in French planning hitherto has been a negotiated incomes policy, since the basis for a dialogue between government and unions has never existed. Thus the plan is in a sense an attempt to bridge the institutional lacunae in French society, to establish a consensus on national objectives which the parliamentary system has hitherto been unable to provide, to give social reform the kind of impetus which can head off extremism.

That is the first objective. The second is to provide industrialists with a general forecast of where the economy is believed to be going, which they may either accept or reject. The third is to activate, as it were, the various instruments at the disposal of the state—sources of preferential credits, public purchases, regional development aid, research grants, etc.—to steer enterprises in the direction the government wishes them to go.

Through the mechanism of the plan, which is known to reflect the views of the President, France has been able to develop an economic strategy which is now apparently to be broadened into a social policy strategy as well. History shows that the planners in France are fallible, as elsewhere. Where they have been successful, it has been primarily because those who frame the plan (French plans are basically constructed on a 'bottom-up' rather than a 'top-down' basis) are essentially representatives of the same élites, who share common assumptions and who operate a very effective communication system. This approach has the weakness that if it goes wrong, as in 1968, there is no 'fail-safe' mechanism available to correct it. But for most of the postwar period the system has worked.

Perhaps the real test of the French planning system will come when the trade unions start to play a central, rather than a peripheral, part in it. In the meantime the French Seventh Plan, despite its considerable limitations, offers the kind of social and economic blueprint towards which a British Government and NEDC might reasonably aspire.

NOTES

1 The White Paper on the approach to industrial strategy was presented to Parliament in November 1975.

2 It might also, in the opinion of some NEDC members, strengthen Neddy's position *vis-à-vis* the Treasury.

3 When Mr Healey, in his April 1976 Budget, made certain tax concessions conditional on TUC acceptance of income restraints in Stage 2 of the counter-inflation policy, there was a widespread feeling that this was somehow improper. The TUC was being made the final arbiter on tax concessions affecting many people who were not even union members. The TUC, on the other hand, felt it was being trapped. The Chancellor was publicly forcing the unions to accept responsibility for policy commensurate with their real power. In fact, the gamble paid off. The unions accepted Stage 2, and the public got its tax cuts. In most Continental countries, this procedure would have been accepted as normal. It would have seemed rather strange if a government had introduced major tax changes *without* prior consultation with the major interest groups in the society, both inside and outside Parliament. The fetish of Budget secrecy in Britain is among the many institutional obstacles to sound economic planning.

4 Another important question which arises from time to time is whether other interests besides the CBI and TUC should be represented on the NEDC. The British Institute of Management and the Association of British Chambers of Commerce have both applied for formal representation, and have been turned down. Consumers are now represented not only by the Minister for Consumer Affairs but by one of the independent members. The City and agriculture are formally represented, as well as private and nationalised industry and the trade unions. The more powerful NEDC becomes, the more other interests will certainly seek representation.

5 Perhaps the communication gap has been not so much between industry and its sponsor departments as between these and the Treasury. The Treasury has always until recently been a somewhat introverted department, whose over-riding power went with a certain secretiveness and remoteness. There are signs that under Mr Healey, with his keen interest in the details of industrial policy, this has changed.

6 Bacon and Eltis analyse the persistent failure to divert adequate resources to industrial investment due to the other pressures on output through the successive initiatives of Messrs Maudling, Brown, Jenkins and Barber.

Mr Maudling began the process by giving excessive stimulus in his 1963 reflationary Budget to public sector investment (up by 20% a year) and consumer durables (cars and houses). Non-industrial employment increased three times as fast between 1961 and 1964 as the Green Book had anticipated. Industrial investment did rise as a result of the Maudling boom, but typically it took a long time to get going and peaked in 1965, at a time when there was great pressure on resources. The 1966 cutback therefore hit industrial investment at a critical time. This was a repetition of the 'stop-go-stop' phenomenon of the 1950s.

In fact the main casualty of the Maudling era was exports, which fell from 15% to 12½% of national output. Consumption also dropped slightly in percentage terms, while the biggest rise was in non-industrial investment (from 14.3% to over 18% of national output). There was a marginal net shift of resources from the balance of payments to industrial investment.

The George Brown era produced only a very marginal shift of resources—a slight net movement from public to private investment (the 1965 investment boom) and a tiny recovery in the proportion of output going to exports.

The major changes occurred under Roy Jenkins and Anthony Barber. Under Jenkins 1% of industrial production was diverted to the balance of payments, but from the long-term point of view this was more than offset by a 2% drop in the proportion of output going to industrial investment (mainly in the nationalised industries). On the employment side, the net movement of manpower into the non-market sector gathered pace, and the total proportion of national output going to the non-market sector rose from 45% in 1966 to 51½% in 1970. This was at the expense, not only of investment but also of consumer spending, which was held back in real terms until the wage explosion started in 1969.

The allocation of resources worsened sharply between 1970 and 1973, owing to the remarkable expansion of the public sector. Consumption and investment outside industry jumped from under 66% of national output to nearly 74%, net investment in manufacturing industry fell from 6.2% to 3.5% and net exports of manufactures (exports of manufactures less imports of manufactures) from 11.4% to 5.9%, consumption by industrial workers remaining roughly constant. The movement of manpower into the non-market public sector accelerated, the 'dash for growth' being financed by an uncontrolled expansion of the money supply. This extra money did not go into industrial investment, but into more profitable outlets outside the productive economy —property especially. The property boom and related phenomena not only pushed up living costs and diverted resources from more urgent national needs, but acted as a social irritant when the government had to deal with trade unions. In the scramble for scarce financial resources during the 1973 boom the private industrial sector was hamstrung by the government's two-way squeeze on profits (via taxes and the price code), and thus industrial investment lagged despite the high volume of demand. The deterioration in Britain's economic structure, slow up to 1970, gathered pace thereafter. By the time Labour returned to office in 1974 net manufacturing investment had fallen to less than 4% of national production. Two years later the position was still basically unchanged.

# Conclusion

The conclusions of this study can be stated very briefly. The main positive lesson to be drawn from the Neddy experiment is that, given the nature of modern industrial society, decisions on economic and industrial policy (and, I would add, social policy) are likely to be most successful if considered in a tripartite framework. Second, detailed quantitative forecasts are not essential for the framing of macro-economic policy, but without some framework of forecasting such policies are likely to go wrong. Third, micro-economic policies, however good, are no substitute for a coherent macro-economic strategy. But a macro-economic strategy which does not take account of realities at micro level is unlikely to be fully effective. There are many issues which need to be dealt with at micro level which collectively can make a considerable impact on the overall economic prospects of the nation. To that extent the 1975-6 industrial strategy seems to offer better long-term prospects than its predecessors, though it will clearly need to evolve over the years.

We waste much time discussing the morality of planning, the alleged conflict between planning and the market economy, the extent to which plans should be indicative (merely indicating what is happening and likely to happen), normative (trying to influence people to act in a certain way) or coercive (replacing market incentives by government edict, compelling people to act in a way they would otherwise not). As I have indicated in this book, I believe that any plan which ignores or seeks to work against market forces is likely to fail. On the other hand, no large organisation—least of all a government—which has to commit resources far into the future can afford not to forecast and to seek to develop a strategy for the best use of its resources. It follows that any plan must be more than purely indicative, at least in so far as it involves the public sector; and any government seeks to influence the behaviour of the private sector through its tax and legislative system and other instruments. Thus any plan in a modern democracy is bound to have a normative element as regards the private sector, and a coercive element as regards the public sector (where government gives the orders anyway).

The argument should therefore not be about 'whether' to plan, but about 'how'. And the most important element in any plan is not the numbering—there is a remarkable, but not very surprising, similarity about the forecasts and targets in each of the planning documents described in this book (as the Appendices illustrate)—but the strategy. This is what the argument should be about: what is the strategy to be followed and, once agreed, how are we to make it happen? The evidence of this book suggests that it is precisely on this point that successive British governments have failed to provide the leadership and the coherent thought required, by refusing to make the necessary choices between mutually incompatible alternatives. To this extent the planning exercises carried out between 1961 and 1976 have been charades rather than serious exercises in national growth and survival. It remains to be seen whether the 1976 industrial strategy will have a happier outcome.

What we have to recognise is that there is no new panacea waiting to be applied, no magic formula which will resolve all our problems, no new hitherto unthought-of path to be taken. The most promising solution to our difficulties is through starting to practise what we have been preaching. We should start to plan.

# Appendices

Appendices 1 to 6 inclusive are heavily edited (by me) versions of papers prepared by the Neddy Office for the Council on the main planning documents from 1963 onwards. I have included them here because I did not want to overload the text in the main part of the book with detailed comparisons of planning documents which may be of less interest to the general reader than an account of what actually happened. The reader who is interested in the detailed content of the different planning documents, and how they compared one with another, will find useful additional material in the Appendices. But for the general reader they are optional rather than essential reading.

Appendix 7 is the full text of the White Paper presented to Parliament by the government after the November 1975 meeting of the NEDC at Chequers. It is reproduced here in full as the best statement yet published of the thinking behind the 1976 approach to industrial strategy by government and NEDC.

# Appendix 1: Growth of the UK Economy to 1966, NEDC, February 1963 (the Green Book)

This document was prepared between March 1962 and February 1963 and was the first task of the newly constituted Council. It set out a 4% per annum growth objective.

The report discussed the implications of 4% growth per annum at the industrial level (baianced growth), and the implications for macro-economic policies, e.g. for manpower, investment and the balance of payments.

The objective was to monitor industry's corporate plans, to assess the implications of the postulated 4% growth and to identify problems impeding higher growth. The whole concept was to study the industrial dimensions of national growth on demand for products. How the economy was to be shifted on to this growth path was outside the terms of reference. The availability of adequate resources was assumed.

The seventeen industries surveyed said that if the economy as a whole grew at 4% then they could grow at 4.8% per annum. The rest of the economy then only needed to grow at 3.5% per annum to achieve the overall 4%.

Part II of the 1963 document considered the implications for macro-economic aspects of the economy. Manpower was expected not to constitute a major constraint. Shortages of skilled workers and technical workers could be avoided only by increased scientific training. Productivity growth was seen as stemming from investment not from more efficient use of resources and was expected to accelerate. Productivity growth would show itself directly in output terms and indirectly in quality terms. Research and technical development would raise productivity. No mention was made of the role of micro-demand management in achieving economies of scale and hence productivity increase.

Concentration was expected to lead to productivity growth. Advisory services were expected to help by incorporating known technology into actual techniques of production. Construction productivity was to rise as client, architect and contractor rationalised their relationships and fluctuations in demand were reduced.

Management consultants were expected to increase their market penetration and raise productivity in their train. Productivity was expected to rise as public education and training expanded.

Technical change was seen as a key factor. The fruits of productivity growth stemming from technical change were expected to accrue from the application of already known basic research. The UK was chided for its slowness off the mark in the application of development work. This was partly attributed to scientific illiteracy of management, partly to financial considerations and to the short-term unprofitability of modernisation. Small and medium-sized companies were seen as too slow to adopt advanced management techniques.

Research may have been neglected as too risky, too long term, or too socially (rather than privately) productive for the firm. Some industries or firms may have been so backward that outside assistance was essential.

Structure was seen as a possible obstacle to development and incidental concentration might raise productivity.

The absence of any adequate study of likely trends in consumer demand was remarked upon as a deficiency to be rectified 'before long'.

Investment in manufacturing industries covered by the study was forecast to fall over the period (1961-6) especially on account of a fall in iron and steel industry investment. The rest of manufacturing industry's investment would have to rise quite strongly at 7.7% per annum to satisfy the overall estimate which was of a 3.4% per annum growth. Ex-post, only 2.6% per annum was realised 1960-72. In general, capacity utilisation was expected to rise.

Investment other than in manufacturing and dwellings was estimated to grow at 6.5% per annum in real terms, but investment in dwellings was estimated at a slower rate, even slower than the postulated GDP rate of 4%.

The combination of higher total domestic investment and the achievement of a balance-of-payments surplus implied an increase in the savings ratio. Personal savings were not expected to increase as rapidly as in the past and corporate savings were assumed to remain at the 1961 proportion of corporate income. The public corporations were to have large increases in their savings resulting from the (successful) operation of policies of the 1961 White Paper on the Financial Obligations of Nationalised Industries (Cmnd 1337). The government, on the assumptions used and the dependent calculations, would have had an increased surplus associated with lower interest rates and more stable prices.

THE BALANCE OF PAYMENTS

This was the era of great concentration on the balance of payments. The improvement was needed to repay old debts but mostly to finance long-term lending to underdeveloped countries to the extent of 1% of UK national income.

Exports were to expand at a calculated 5% by an improvement in UK competitiveness. Entry into the EEC was not assumed but was seen as beneficial should it occur. It was appreciated that the task was formidable but was thought to be feasible provided world exports of manufactures were strong and Britain did not lose competitiveness. The direction of British trade, depending on more slowly growing markets, was seen as a handicap. Both this factor and the commodity composition of UK trade were dismissed as significant explanations of our declining share of world export of manufactures.

The low rate of UK investment in manufacturing industry and slow rate of growth in productivity were recognised but simply *assumed* to change for the better in the future.

PHASING

The document recognised the problem that growth in the first year of the period was below the postulated trend. The problem of getting back on trend was discussed in terms of more school leavers and immigrants, productivity growth and faster investment especially towards the end of the period. Faster investment might spring from increased capital allowances of November 1962 and the postulated lower rate of interest. Oldfashioned multiplier theory was adduced to suggest that if the UK achieved increased investment then consumers' expenditure would rise as the growth programme generated income.

Hopefully, increased efficiency in the use of capital equipment and faster investment would avoid marked changes in the pattern of demand, but demand management in general and with respect to special categories would be required.

The document concluded by recognising that there were problems to be tackled but tripartite commitment and determination would be a vital requirement.

# Appendix 2: Conditions favourable to faster growth (1963) (the Orange Book)

This document discussed points which emerged from the industrial inquiry of *Growth of the United Kingdom Economy to 1966*. It discussed such topics as the relevance of education to growth; labour mobility, redundancy and growth; balance-of-payments policies; taxation; level of demand; prices and incomes and tripartism.

The positive functional dependence of economic growth on education was asserted as a dogma. Expenditure on education was estimated to rise from 4.4% of GNP in 1961-2 to 4.9% in 1963-4. American work was cited on the social rate of return enjoyed by expenditure on education.

In the long term, it was argued, education promoted technical change. The embodiment of research into technology may, however, have to be stimulated. Cross-fertilisation between university research and industrial application was called for, as was the need for management to have qualifications in science and technology. Steps must be taken to avert shortages of technicians.

The developments of sociology can help to raise productivity and the design and layout of plants could be improved to gain productivity growth. The industrial application of defence research should be promoted. A dialogue was promised between the parties of government and industry and the council for Scientific and Industrial Research.

A declaration of faith in management for productivity was made. Managers must not become 'merely competent administrators'. Innate skills are not implantable, but practical and theoretical training should take place, especially for those already on the job. Managers should be *au fait* with operational research and appreciate the importance of human and industrial relations. (The dichotomy is in the text.)

Managers should have a better working knowledge of other languages. Financial and operating ratios should be studied and inter-firm comparisons should be made and noted. Managers of small businesses especially were expected to benefit from inter-firm comparisons. Management education needed to be assisted by offering industrial experience to technical teachers.

The case for the extension of graduate business education in the UK on the American lines was made; on the whole, the postgraduate, post-experience audience was selected.

Despite efforts to raise the supply, there were likely to be shortages of skilled craftsmen. Adult training and re-training should be further promoted. The government training centres needed to be expanded and this was being done. The allowances paid to trainees were tax free and, as at September 1962, were brought close to the minimum unskilled wage level.

It was suggested that greater variety in courses should be preferred. A rapidly growing economy would enjoy attitudes of mind conducive to the acceptance of expanded supplies of skilled workers. Both the Swedish Labour Market Board and the USA Government provided about 1% per annum of the skilled workforce and 1.4% of the non-agricultural workforce over a three-year period respectively.

The statutory boards of Cmnd 1892 are welcomed in the report. A thorough overhaul of the apprenticeship system was advocated, associated with a study of training arrangements for young worker entrants in other than the traditional crafts prepared for by the apprenticeship system. Attention should be paid primarily to the areas of engineering and construction.

MOBILITY AND REDUNDANCY

Reallocation of labour resources was discussed and the policy measures likely to be needed to supplement the market. Measures to promote labour mobility included cushioning the hardships of redundancy, better housing, transfer and resettlement allowances, training facilities for displaced workers and financial provisions to tide over until re-employment. Measures should promote acquiescence in response to market forces by workers and avoid labour hoarding by employers.

Manpower planning could be developed to avoid unnecessary redundancies. Necessary redundancies would be made more acceptable by the policies mentioned backed up by long notices and phased release.

Housing was seen as the largest single factor affecting labour mobility. Exchange schemes for council houses should be promoted and local authorities should have a special 'industrial mobility' subsidy to build houses for transferred workers. Ministry of Labour resettlement scheme grants and allowances were too low.

Private occupational pensions schemes were seen to impede mobility of employment, especially for higher grade staff.

Earnings-related benefit schemes should be introduced. (This has, of course, been done.)

Company redundancy schemes were criticised as encouraging labour hoarding. Industry redundancy schemes presented difficulties for declining industries. A state graduated unemployment scheme should be established (done). Alternatively a national redundancy fund more narrowly defined than unemployment in general was a possibility, but was rejected as inequitable and cumbersome to administer.

REGIONAL QUESTIONS

Drawing into employment the unemployed and the economically inactive in the disadvantaged regions could contribute helpfully to growth. How to achieve this was the problem. Perhaps incentives should be bigger to diminish the reliance upon constraint of development elsewhere. Such policies could yield an increment in the workforce of some 0.1% per annum over the five years and this would reduce the productivity increase needed elsewhere in the economy. Successful policies would reduce the burden of unemployment benefit and national assistance and create a higher revenue.

Expansion in prosperous regions shifts labour from lower-productivity to higher-productivity activities but expansion in the less prosperous regions brings into production labour which was previously economically idle.

The counter-argument of free labour mobility to more prosperous regions was rejected as creating social costs of migration and congestion and leaving the less prosperous regions even less viable.

The industrial development certificate system (IDCs) was criticised as leading to the abandonment of some projects. The system should fall away before adequate positive policies. The positive system should be well publicised for industrial planning both by national companies and by multi-nationals.

Cost disadvantages of locating in the less prosperous regions were likely to be felt worst in the early years of establishment. Incentives should therefore more than outweigh this. The result may be achieved either by capital incentives or by some form of regional labour subsidy (a flat rate labour subsidy is now payable).

The less profitable regions might be better served by the identification and promotion of growth points. The growth point concept was not only relevant to the less prosperous regions.

The provision of better public infrastructure and social capital would provide a direct stimulus to the regional economies.

The regional problem was seen to be best mitigated by a high level of demand in the country as a whole. In so far as regional imbalance is corrected, the performance of the economy with respect to inflation and the balance of payments in a strong demand situation is improved. Thus better regional development means less severe 'stops' in the 'stop-go' cycle.

Other West European countries tend to prefer positive incentives to locate in the less favoured regions rather than negative controls operating in the national growth points.

BALANCE OF PAYMENTS POLICIES

Expansion in the UK has always been checked when the balance of payments ran into intolerable deficits. A substantial deficit should be tolerable for a year or so by recourse to the IMF and by borrowing against the government's holdings of dollar securities. But under the then holding 'adjustable peg' system of fixed exchange rates, a run on reserves could not be tolerated. Every opportunity to increase the total of international liquidity ought to be taken in the interest of the growth of trade.

Methods to strengthen the balance of payments might include: term loans, special considerations in regional development to firms with export potential, import saving potential or multinationals. Fiscal discrimination in favour of foreign incomers was touched upon, but on the whole rejected.

The contribution of shipping to our invisibles was to be looked at by the Ministry of Transport's Shipping Advisory Panel. Public expenditure abroad, especially on defence, should be kept in check. VAT ought to be introduced.

Other last stage measures could include: finance for exports, quantitative import control, funding of sterling balances and restriction of private investment abroad. Most of these are either irrelevant under floating exchange rates or inconsistent with liberalisation of trade (the French had export subsidies and import levies before 1959). In general, the document did not favour jeopardising our trading relationships.

The document rejected the avenue of avoiding balance-of-payments problems by restricting growth. Productivity growth was seen as depending primarily upon output growth. In general, attributes of the economy which led to growth led also to strong exports.

The document concluded, incontrovertibly, that the only acceptable and effective measures to improve the external balance are those which lead to increased international competitiveness.

## TAXATION

The total tax burden in the UK relative to national income was not out of line with foreign competitors, but their systems were different. Payroll taxes were common in Continental countries whereas in the UK taxes on employment were flat-rate; VAT was general on the Continent and the CAP system was different.

Investment allowances were thought to be the more beneficial to growth the greater the confidence of industry that they would persist.

The stabilisation of investment by some scheme such as the Swedish 'tax free profits for investment reserves' scheme or the machine tool industry's 'tax allowances for interest-bearing investment certificates' was commended.

The rating system's impact upon industry came in for criticism in industrial consultations but not much was made of this.

## DEMAND MANAGEMENT

A high and stable level of demand was recognised to ease regional problems and to reduce the level of productivity growth necessary to achieve target output.

Up to a point output rises with demand. Even after bottlenecks of capacity constraints reduce output per head, total output still grows with effective demand for a while.

Raised output permits investment to be raised also. The pressure upon capacity encourages investment decisions to be made. Shortages of labour reinforce the attraction of the investment opportunity as not only can more output be produced profitably, but costs may be reduced by new capital equipment being more labour saving (assuming it is not then overmanned). Investment decisions were recognised to be highly sensitive to the pressure of demand.

High demand may promote labour hoarding and thus reduce efficiency, but low demand inhibits innovation and makes labour fearful of redundancy.

Structural change may not be impeded by high demand, as is often argued, as labour is released with worker-acquiescence when demand is high and new jobs seem safer to take up.

Importance was attached to reducing the rise in money incomes associated with a given unemployment rate. Measures which might contribute towards this were the reduction in the regional disparity in unemployment rates; increased labour mobility; and improved matching of supply and demand for particular skills. The level of demand impinges on the balance of payments via imports fluctuations rather than via exports fluctuations. The document rejected both the theory that exports are encouraged by strong home markets and the reverse, that high pressure of domestic demand diverts output on to the home market.

Certainly fluctuating but high levels of demand were likely to be worse for the balance of payments in the short run when there is little in hand. In the longer term high levels of demand would yield productivity growth acceleration and the balance-of-payments constraint might cease to bite.

All in all, the macro management of the economy should seek moderately high capacity utilisation and steady but not excessive growth.

## PRICES AND INCOMES

The lack of international competitiveness was adduced as an important reason for the falling UK share of world exports of manufactures. This lack of competitiveness was attributed to faster growth in labour money earnings and slower growth in productivity than our competitors. (The theme seems remarkably more like a scenario of secular decline now than a description of medium-term difficulties.)

Additionally, trade liberalisation and independence for formerly dependent territories had removed the UK's sheltered position in certain markets.

Money incomes in the UK must not rise as rapidly in the future (1963 onwards) as had been the case in the recent past (1948-61). Only by controlling the rate of growth in money incomes and succeeding in the strategy for expansion could real incomes grow.

The social acceptance of incomes restraint as being in the interests of recipients of incomes from employment in general was thought to be important.

## GOVERNMENT MANAGEMENT

Government commitment to growth priority was important. Public sector investment programmes should be more reliably planned in the longer term. Strong government must preclude wrecking behaviour by small groups of sectional interests.

Management must rethink its attitudes and improve the quality of its investment planning and handle successfully the faster rise in productivity. Labour relations were first and foremost a managerial responsibility. Best-practice techniques must be more widely used.

Restrictive practices had no useful role in a growing economy.

Industrial wage structures needed rationalisation and this could best be tackled in a growth context.

# Appendix 3: The Growth of the Economy (March 1964)

This document studied the way in which the *Growth in the UK Economy to 1966* (1963) document appeared to be working out and was presented to the Council thirteen months after the first document. As it must have taken, say, four weeks to edit and prepare for the Council, the judgements must have been made effectively in the fourth quarter of 1963.

In response to the 4% objective, public sector current expenditure had reached the level required in *Growth to 1966* and public sector fixed capital formation, especially on building and works, had exceeded it.

The investment plans of the electricity industry had been remodelled in the light of the 4% growth programme (which was to result in excess capacity subsequently). The Post Office had also raised the scale of its investment plans in response to 4% growth.

Private investment, except in e.g. chemicals, looked like falling short of target but (hopefully) this was expected only to balance the public sector overshoot.

Skilled labour supply continued to cause anxiety, but the required rate of growth of labour productivity gave the document's drafters more anxiety than, apparently, the private and public industries consulted.

The balance of payments already gave grounds for anxiety. Imports were rising faster than had been felt appropriate, but it was hoped to salve the export requirement of 5% by lowering the external balance objective from a surplus of £50 million (prices as in *Growth to 1966* presumably, but not specified) to a balance. Additionally, target capital exports were reduced. There was no attempt to analyse the increase in imports causally except through growth rate variations in stockbuilding and cost competitiveness of import substitutes.

Output, employment and productivity growth were deemed rather more than satisfactory during 1963 to compensate for slow growth in 1961 and 1962, and this was mainly attributed to the fuller use of resources.

The outlook was then for demand to increase at a fast rate involving greater investment, public and private, in fixed capital and in stocks; public and private consumption should be strong and exports were expected to grow with world trade but not as fast as imports. Productivity growth was expected to conform to the programmed trend.

Capacity constraints were expected to trim down the growth in output, but a plea was put in for any demand dampening to avoid abrupt operation.

Investment in manufactures gave grounds for anxiety. It was thought that shortages of skilled labour might prevent output growth targets being satisfied in some industries unless re-equipment investment took place to raise labour productivity. The Council thought that industry might not appreciate the significance of capital allowances.

Several industries showed scepticism of the attainability of the growth target over the period. This attitude jeopardised the investment targets and was to be dealt with by convincing business that the 'stop' of policy was a device of the past.

Efficiency in stock management in the UK was thought to be low and the EDCs were to study how stockholding could be reduced.

Private savings were the subject of some concern in view of the need to release resources for investment, if the investment, which was faltering, was to materialise. Measures to promote private saving might be needed or a budget surplus to compensate might be needed.

Construction had a large task including a heavy house-building programme; this industry was seen as needing more training, recruitment, and new methods to get the output and productivity growth.

The Council was anxious to review the progress made on labour planning, training, mobility and security.

Regional balance in the UK was thought to be improved but further improvement might well be needed.

The balance of payments was an anxiety area. If trouble developed here the safeguarding of the balance of payments could force a domestic deflation which would prevent the growth target being reached. Imports of manufactures were a special worry. In this connection cost competitiveness was vital and inflation a danger.

The incomes policy of perfection was quietly demanded in that profits, wages and salaries should not rise faster than output. An economy seeking demand-led growth must exercise vigilance on prices or international non-competitiveness may preclude attainment of the target.

Generally, industrial modernisation was thought to be lagging and the necessary investment would need more UK saving to finance it.

Trend growth can only come from productivity growth and this must come in a context of successful counter-cyclical policy. Growth, once achieved over a reasonable span, would become self-perpetuating.

The 1961-to-4th-quarter-1963 out-turn was compared with the growth target trend for production, manpower, productivity, consumers' expenditure and public consumption, investment, savings and balance of payments. With respect to GDP it was quite clear that the first three years of the six-year period were below target trend. Therefore, for the target trend to be realised the last three years would have had to have exceeded trend.

Part III of this document contained the results of checking out the no-path seventeen-industry inquiry estimates for 1966 in the light of their experiences and current expectations. Additionally, electrical and mechanical engineering, non-ferrous metals and food processing were added. A high degree of industrial co-operation was obtained.

# Appendix 4: The National Plan (September 1965)

The National Plan was a 'growthmanship' document. The objective was to break out from the vicious circle of low growth by removing underlying weaknesses. The central challenge was seen as the problem of simultaneously achieving a surplus on the balance of payments and rapid growth.

The study was very action-oriented. A check-list of actions required, cross-referenced to sections, was given. The appropriate body to take the action was designated. The action check-list was divided into balance of payments, industrial efficiency, manpower policy, regional policy, public spending and periodic reviews.

The role of the NEDC and the EDCs was to *identify* opportunities for gains from efficiency and growth at the national level and to exploit them through the EDCs.

The EDCs were expected to develop a dialogue between themselves. Topics could be jointly pursued by EDCs, such as import savings, standardisation, rationalisation, movement of exports, industrial co-operation.

Government had promoted competition by monopoly and resale price maintenance legislation. Government supported research and development in science and technology. The specific shortage of engineers was recognised and steps were promised to rectify this. Government would, it was averred, support projects to demonstrate the technical and economic benefits of automatic operation and project control.

Labour productivity was to be promoted by a strategy of regional and manpower policies. EDCs would be agencies to assist in this by forecasting labour bottlenecks, improving labour planning, improving the allocation of labour to higher-productivity jobs and to tackle restrictive practices.

Management was to be made more effective by exploiting opportunities for management education and use of appropriate consultants. EDCs would also examine aspects of management. Investment appraisal would incorporate a barrage of special techniques.

The improvement in industrial efficiency was the necessary pre-condition for the success of the Plan. The challenge was seen to be formidable.

Investment was thought to lie at the heart of the Plan. (Somehow) the Plan was to ensure that the investment was carried out and was correctly located.

A discussion of the nationalised industries' investment plans was tentative, but the various sectors were discussed in a similar way to White Papers on public expenditure.

OVERALL

The merit of this work has been obscured by:

(a) *too high a growth rate* for credibility;
(b) *no wedge approach*, so that if growth was not at 4% the Plan seemed worthless;
(c) *no reference or base case* on how the economy would be expected to develop anyway;
(d) *no clear strategy* for pushing the economy from (c) to the 4% case;
(e) *no mechanism* for implementing the strategy;
(f) *no path* which would have enabled analysts to see how under-performance in the early years would need to be compensated for later;
(g) *no revealed methodology* so that when the 4% no longer held, the reader could not use the structure.

Therefore when the 4% was not reached the Plan was abandoned and with this abandonment planning became less respectable.

# Appendix 5: The Task Ahead—Economic Assessment to 1972

This assessment was prepared by government as a basic text for consultations within the Council and with industry, using EDCs. Government took responsibility for the views of the document. Publication was intended to admit Parliament and public to the government/Neddy exercise. This document set out government policies in relation to tasks and prospects. An advance over earlier documents was the inclusion of both a better and a worse potential out-turn.

The notion of planning presented is of a continuous forward exercise of foresight evolving practical responses to the conditions foreseen. This document is differentiated from the 1965 National Plan by being not a 'plan' but a 'planning document'. It was to be a medium-term (1969-72) assessment of demand prospects and resource availability, to provide a macro framework for resource-based discussions at the industry level.

Flexibility of methodology with respect to new developments was to be sought so that the document was not invalidated by the first disturbances to the assumed scenario. The need for revision was to be minimised.

The objective was still good growth, which was seen to depend upon the achievement of satisfactory external balance and an improvement in domestic resource allocation. The document was presented as provisional, incomplete and subject to consultations.

Planning was seen to require:

(a) analysis of the present and past trends;
(b) forecasting in uncertainty with due regard to possible variations in out-turn;
(c) government/industry discussions;
(d) study of constraints and hindrances;
(e) action to overcome (d) to improve performance.

Performance could be improved without quantification, but the 'numbers game' was believed to be beneficial to private decision making. Hopefully, this might assist the private sector to accept government's expenditure.

This was seen as the era of corporate planning associated with better planning by government and nationalised industries. All needed the framework. Targetry in the style of 1963, 1964 and 1965 was rejected, but so was policy without co-ordination. This document was to be the basis of the co-ordination.

The controversy about whether to plan was seen as sterile. Plans were being made, the debate should be about their co-ordination and characteristics. This document was to be seen as highly provisional and as abstaining from any single rate of growth. In practice, the industrial assessment did have a single rate of growth, presumably as the practical difficulties of component wedges are great. If the total is to lie within a given wedge and a wedge exists for each component conditional upon what goes on elsewhere, everything becomes difficult to handle.

The macro 'wedge' is a trend wedge and was not to be interpreted as containing or representing the path. Unfortunately, there are great difficulties with medium-term trend planning. We plan with the trend but live on the path; not all find the notional adjustment easy.

General priorities were specified:

*First* an improvement of the external balance into surplus.
*Second* a drive for competitive efficiency by identifying opportunity areas for resource shifts, improvement in productivity and money income restraint to keep down unit costs.
*Third* higher resource utilisation including better regional balance.

Growth was seen as achievable only if the three priority objectives were satisfied in parallel.

The proper office of government was to set the scene and create the climate. Effective tripartism was the essential process which would enable economic recovery to take place. The planning process was seen to be a continuing one, subject to repeated revisions in an ongoing consultative monitoring of the UK's economic efficiency and development.

THE STRATEGY AND PROSPECT

The prime aim of policy was to convert the external payment deficit into a surplus of the order of £500 million and continue this to retire debt amounting to more than £2,000 million. The assumption was that EEC membership would not be achieved during the assessment period.

The swing of resources into the external sector was to be achieved through structural change and a general increase in efficiency. The National Plan's 'check-list of action' was approved and monitored.

To these ends labour was being redeployed; management education was being fostered; R & D promoted; standardisation and quality sought etc., etc.

This was the era of investment grants instead of allowances, and much hope was placed in this change for manufacturing investment. Measures which included the Industrial Expansion Act were to provide selective help for industry.

The policy on productivity, prices and incomes was designed to produce a competitive economy with stable costs and prices to take advantage of the benefits of the 1967 devaluation of 14.3%. There seemed every confidence of success.

Factors which might limit growth were seen as the possible failure of productive potential to grow as required and possible failure on the external front. External failure could be beyond our control, e.g. a recession in world trade; or culpable, stemming from e.g. failure to seize opportunities, failure of efficiency in keeping costs down, excessive pressure to consume.

The out-turn for the economy was presented as dependent upon what the world did to us and with what drive we produced.

The illustrative part of this work was based upon 3½% per annum, but the detailed industrial estimates were based on 3¼% per annum growth.

EMPLOYMENT

Lowest possible unemployment was a major objective, but this was defined in a market context as that rate at which labour markets are in 'proper balance'. Excess demand in some labour markets was to be avoided, and the supply balance of skills must be kept appropriate by trimming the training programmes.

A strong plea was made to understand that world demand would take up cost-competitive British goods, so that fast productivity growth would not work workers out of jobs.

USE OF RESOURCES

A feature of the strategy was to be control in real terms of public sector expenditure at a low rate of growth except for public investment. Personal consumption must be restrained in the early stages. The fruit of success was to be consumption tomorrow.

An under-performance by the economy would mean less public expenditure. An over-performance would permit an increase in personal and collective consumption in some ratio to be considered.

THE NEXT STAGE

Special detailed consideration of *The Task Ahead* was proposed for selected industries. EDCs were to be only one avenue of consultations. Government would continue to treat with trade associations and firms. Consultation within the public sector would be by the normal continuing process.

It was intended that this round of consultations should be the beginning of a continuing process.

# Economic Prospects to 1972 – A Revised Assessment (May 1970)

This was a government document prepared in January 1970 to take account of the consultations with industry which took place during 1969 through the EDCs and other consultative bodies and changes in the economy since the publication of *The Task Ahead*. These consultations resulted in a number of industry reports which assessed their industry's prospects to 1972, examined possible constraints to improved performance and recommended action to be taken by government and industry.

This document was prepared to assist the Council to take an overall view of the planning exercise of the *Economic Assessment*. This exercise was characterised by being an industrial essay into corporate planning on consistent and externally provided macro assumptions. It did not purport to change what the economy was proposing to do, but sought to help it to be more successful at its own economic strategy.

This *Revised Assessment* document was, as *The Task Ahead*, presented not as a plan but as a basis for further forward planning and (independent) decision taking by government and industry. Not to be a plan was an important attribute of acceptability at that stage. The document ('Green Paper') contained a commitment to the joint government and industrial development of the consultative planning process.

PRODUCTIVITY, OUTPUT AND EMPLOYMENT

The pressure of demand over the projected period was revised downwards, but the drawing-in of unused capacity in the regions by increased demand was still thought feasible. Success in macro and regional demand planning by government would permit the whole economy to operate closer to productive potential and hence increase growth. But this success was not, apparently, to be presumed.

For policy purposes the projected growth rate in GDP was dropped from the range of 3-4% a year to the lower range of 3-3¾% per annum.

BALANCE OF PAYMENTS

Here the outlook was improved compared with the picture fifteen months earlier. Thus the required performance for visible trade was eased.

However, the import growth assumptions of *The Task Ahead* needed to take account of an increased propensity to import finished manufactures and capital goods and the results of the consultations with the EDCs for engineering, motor and chemical industries which raised the import projections of *The Task Ahead*.

*The Task Ahead* postulated a basic case export growth requirement of 5.8% per annum on average between 1967 and 1972. The revision substituted 6.4% per annum from 1969 to 1972 which would imply 4.25% per annum growth between 1969 and 1972.

Concern was expressed that the higher export requirements (exceeding also the EDCs' export forecasts) should be seen to be realistic, as otherwise the engineering industries in particular might not expand capacity and exports might be lost from supply constraints.

The EDC exercises apparently adopted the view that only a steadily growing home market could lead to the creation of new capacity without which the export performance could disappoint. The motor industry, in particular, advanced the 'home and export markets are complementary' view, but the machine tools EDC saw the home and export markets as competitive for output unless capacity could be increased.

USE OF RESOURCES

The document acknowledged the satisfactory transition from deficit to surplus on the balance of payments between 1967 and 1969.

The allocation of increased resources from 1969 to 1972 was tentatively described for the basic case and for the higher case. (Unfortunately this was not directly compared with any 'unplanned' reference case, nor was it directly compared with the same growth cases over the longer span of *The Task Ahead*.)

Comparison between the documents indicates that the curtailment of the rate of growth required by public sector consumption was the most striking change; but this did not apparently apply to the social services sector.

The *Revised Assessment* document commented on the tone of the EDCs' responses on investment which are described as 'not very buoyant'.

## POLICY IMPLICATIONS

The government's policy was to take the lower of the possible future resource projections as available on prudential grounds. Demand management would aim to regulate demand to a high and sustainable growth rate, while productivity increases would be pursued by separate instruments.

The vital need in connection with external balance was seen to be to preserve the international competitiveness bought by devaluation and the policies of 1968 and 1969. This must not be jeopardised by an excessive growth of domestic demand.

An economic management balance was seen to be required between increasing manufacturing investment to increase productive capacity further, and over-loading the engineering industries and thus worsening the external position. The priority selected was to be the building-up of capacity by the capital-goods-producing industries.

Such a capacity growth was seen to be dependent upon sustaining business confidence. The EDC reports had special relevance for the long lead-time industries of chemicals and motors, wherein the decisions affecting 1969-72 had already been taken in 1970.

Monetary and credit policies were promised to recognise the importance of adequate cash flow for industrial investment.

## POLICY FOR INDUSTRIAL EFFICIENCY

Priority was claimed for the most efficient use of existing capital equipment.

Additionally, good intentions were expressed with respect to the promotion of labour skills and the expansion of government training centres.

Government policies were to promote industrial efficiency by public procurement policy, by policies for promoting greater industrial specialisation, and by improving standardisation and variety control through the nationalised industries and the local authorities.

Other instruments of policy were to be the IRC, and the proposed Commission for Industry and Manpower to promote efficiency and innovation and to monitor market power.

Efficiency at the company level was to be promoted by sponsored advisory services. The government's own research laboratories would be organised to benefit industry and hence the economy.

EEC membership was looked to for opportunities to reduce unit costs from scale benefits of a large market, and to provide a spur to reduce unit costs from the need to compete successfully.

The consultative planning process of NEDC and EDCs was to be effectively carried forward.

| | Growth 1961-6 (%) | | | National Plan 1964-70 (%) | | | Task Ahead 1967-72 (Basic Plan) (%) | | |
|---|---|---|---|---|---|---|---|---|---|
| | plan (p) | outcome (o) | o/p | plan (p) | outcome (o) | o/p | plan (p) | outcome (o) | o/p |
| GDP | 22 | 16 | 73 | 22 | 14·5 | 58 | 17 | 12 | 71 |
| consumption | 19 | 15 | 79 | 21 | 11 | 52 | 12 | 14·5 | 121 |
| investment | 30 | 24 | 80 | 38 | 23 | 60 | 21 | 11 | 52 |
| public current | 19 | 14 | 74 | 27 | 12 | 44 | 9 | 8 | 89 |
| visible imports | 28 | 19 | 68 | 36 | 39·5 | 109* | 32 | 35 | 109 |
| visible exports | 22 | 19 | 86 | 26 | 29·5 | 113* | 22 | 37 | 168 |
| import growth/ GDP growth | 100 | 119 | | 104 | 203 | | 129 | 308 | |
| investment growth/ consumption growth | 158 | 160 | | 181 | 209 | | 175 | 76 | |
| consumption growth/ GDP growth | 86 | 94 | | 84 | 76 | | 71 | 121 | |

*affected by devaluation

(Reproduced by kind permission of the Oxford University Press from D. K. Stout, 'Government and Private Industry: Medium Term Policies' in *The Economic System in the United Kingdom* edited by D. J. Morris, page 426.)

# Appendix 6: The Industrial Review

The theme of this review, comparable to the balance-of-payments theme of the previous exercise, was to concentrate on the changes in the environment with which selected UK industries would have to deal, especially those resulting from EEC entry. The exercise would be carried out against two 'illustrative' growth rates, but the intention was to do only such numbers work as was essential to give a proper basis for tackling the real issues; effort was to be put into the demand and trade aspects of the work in view of the expected implications of EEC entry. The intention was to improve particularly the analysis of resource requirements, with fuller quantification of manpower implications and a better analysis of investment requirements. As a first step the existing position in each industry was established as a basis for the forward look. Meanwhile, the Treasury were to provide the illustrative growth assumptions and the Office prepared the other inputs for the forward look at demand, trade and output, resource implications and, hence, the issues. This time, instead of reporting each industry's results individually to the Council, the final phase of the work was to be the provision of a separate summary of results. There was great emphasis on doing as much work as possible inside the Office and economising on the time of the consultative committees.

The chief difficulty arose over the growth assumption. The TUC wanted to look at the implications of a 6% growth rate, the CBI did not want to go over 3% and the government's position was between these two rates. Eventually, after much negotiation, 3½% and 5% were settled on. The Treasury then produced a minimal set of projections for the two cases, with not very credible projections for public expenditure and the balance of payments. These were a far cry from *The Task Ahead*, being unsupported by detailed assumptions and (in this respect like *The Task Ahead*) not accompanied by indications of the policies by which they would be achieved. At first, 3½% struck the industrialists as high, but as the exercise went on they accepted it as a reasonable estimate.

The summary was started in the first quarter of 1973 and presented to the Council in July 1973. It provided answers for the industries covered to the questions posed by the Council; in particular, that a 3½% growth could be sustained by these industries provided action was taken on certain constraints, but that 5% presented more serious obstacles, which would take time to overcome and would require a steady build-up to this rate—and, especially, confidence that such a rate could be achieved. Many of the other conclusions were less dependent on the specific growth rates; e.g. the changes in the composition and pattern of demand, trade and output as between industries that would take place over the review period, the recent improvements in manpower productivity and hence a reduction in the number of people required to produce a given output over the review period, and the emphasis on better utilisation and improvement of existing capacity rather than on net expansion of capacity to meet higher growth. EEC entry was not expected to have an immediate impact on trade and output of the review industries until the end of the transition period.

As in the *Economic Assessment*, participants saw the industrial review in two stages; the first consisting of mapping out the ground so that detailed investigation could take place of the issues thrown up, at the second stage. Because of the increasing depth of the analysis made possible by the successive *Economic Assessment* and industrial review, some real progress can now be seen. For example, the clothing, foundries and machine tools Industry Act schemes go back to the work carried out in the review. The paper industry engaged in a critical review of its future strategies on a deeper and longer-term basis than could be carried out in the review itself—a good example of effective action at industrial level.

Opportunity was taken in the industrial review to develop the methodology and techniques, particularly models, appropriate to this kind of work. The comprehensive industrial input-output model was used on an experimental basis and its results used as an internal cross-check. Sector-level models were developed to help with the analysis of textile demand and with the cash implications of the chemical industry's investment programme.

# Appendix 7: An Approach to Industrial Strategy

*The contents of this document were discussed at the meeting of the National Economic Development Council held at Chequers on 5 November 1975.*

FOREWORD BY THE CHANCELLOR OF THE EXCHEQUER AND
THE SECRETARY OF STATE FOR INDUSTRY

1 The British people face immense short-term economic problems in unemployment, inflation and the balance-of-payments deficit. These problems have arisen at regular intervals throughout this century, though rarely in a combination quite so intractable as at present. The exceptional difficulties of Britain's position in the economic recession which grips the whole world is due in large part to the fact that the performance of British industry since the war has been steadily deteriorating under successive governments in comparison with its competitors. So while we tackle immediate problems, we must also get to grips with the long-term weakness of British industry, and relate short-term solutions to the requirements of this task.

2 The task we face is nothing less than to reverse the relative decline of British industry which has been continuous for many years. It is not something we can achieve overnight. The full benefits will only emerge in the long term. But we must start the process now.

3 This document sets out the government's proposals for developing a long-term industrial strategy. We believe that any approach to an industrial strategy must satisfy two conditions. First, it must be realistic and flexible. Our proposals involve a careful analysis of the performance and prospects of individual industries which will be continuously adjusted as experience grows and circumstances change. This analysis does not itself constitute a strategy; it provides a flexible framework within which strategic decisions can be made. Second, it must engage the co-operation and drive of both management and labour in both the private and public sectors. The government emphasises the importance of sustaining a private sector of industry which is vigorous, alert, responsible and profitable. It intends that the public sector should exhibit the same qualities. We intend to achieve the necessary co-operation through regular discussions with representatives of both sides of industry, both at sector and at company level. The decisions which follow the analysis must be made by companies, unions and government.

4 The first results of this approach were reflected in the government's recent

measures to encourage investment on a selective basis. The measures to help investment were chosen after the sort of sectoral analysis which is set out in this paper. They are moreover related to the problems immediately ahead, since they are primarily intended to remove obstacles to the growth of some of our key industries as the world economy recovers. We shall keep the effects of these measures under review and we shall not hesitate to take any further steps that may be necessary, consistent with our over-riding objective of conquering inflation. As we begin to develop a new industrial strategy we shall increasingly be able to plan our short-term measures within a longer-term industrial framework so that short- and long-term measures reinforce one another.

## AN APPROACH TO INDUSTRIAL STRATEGY

### INTRODUCTION

1 Our prime objective must be to become a high output-high wage economy. This can only be achieved by improving our industrial performance and raising the growth of our productive potential.

2 Our unsatisfactory economic performance since the war reflects in large part our failure to deal effectively with our industrial problems by comparison with our competitors. The government is introducing powerful new instruments to tackle these problems, in particular planning agreements and the National Enterprise Board (NEB). These, and the other weapons in our armoury, cannot be used to purposeful effect unless we have a soundly based strategy for manufacturing industry.

3 We need such a strategy also as a guide for manpower planning. In some sectors of industry the pressures of international competition will force some shedding of labour. In others, technological improvements in productivity may mean that as modernisation proceeds, the same or a larger output can be produced with a smaller labour force. It is therefore essential to develop a coherent industrial strategy so that action can be taken in good time by government and companies to expand capacity and increase employment in sectors with good prospects, or in others to take defensive action where this is necessary. Manpower policies like training, re-training and encouragements to mobility must be geared to this strategy.

4 The National Economic Development Council has held a series of discussions about the need for more effective industrial planning. At the August Council meeting the government undertook to produce a paper setting out a new approach to industrial strategy which could then be fully discussed by all the parties. This paper sets out the approach which the government considers likely to be the most realistic and fruitful. It is not a strategy but a programme for developing a strategy which will place responsibility on government, on unions and on management for improving our industrial performance.

### BACKGROUND

5 Manufacturing industry accounts for about 30% of our output and employment and over 80% of our visible exports. Its health is of vital importance to our national economic performance. Our manufacturing industry has not done as well as its competitors. In particular it has not responded adequately to changes in the pattern of world trade and suffers from structural rigidities which show

themselves particularly in bottlenecks both of manpower and components in the early stages of economic upturns. The reasons for our poor performance by international standards have been exhaustively analysed and discussed, not least in the Council and the Economic Development Committees. There is no universal agreement on them. Some important factors, such as an overvalued exchange rate and excessive international responsibilities, may now be less serious. Others, such as a limited supply of labour for manufacturing industry to draw on, are bound to affect Britain more deeply than some of her competitors. But whatever weight may be given to one or the other the main relevant factors are clearly interrelated. They are thought to include:

*Investment*
- (i) a low rate of investment
- (ii) inefficient use of capital, which has resulted in a relatively poor return on new investment
- (iii) poor choice of investment

*Labour*
- (iv) inadequate development of a manpower policy and the consequent regional and sectoral shortages of skilled labour
- (v) low labour productivity reflecting poor management, inadequate consultation, restrictive practices, overmanning and disruption by industrial action
- (vi) attitudes to productivity and labour mobility based on views about appropriate pay and tax structures which reflect long-standing attitudes to relative pay in industry

*Government*
- (vii) sharp and frequent changes of economic regulators to meet the conflicting needs of economic and social priorities, which make it difficult for companies to plan ahead
- (viii) pre-emption of resources by the public sector and by personal consumption to the detriment of industry's investment and export performance
- (ix) government intervention in the pricing, investment and employment policies of the nationalised industries

*Finance*
- (x) a declining rate of industrial profitability
- (xi) imperfections in the capital markets mainly at the medium- and longer-term ends
- (xii) a capital market which does not give priority to the needs of industry.

6 There is no reason to believe that these problems will be solved automatically. Indeed, international factors are likely to make them more difficult—as the developing world sets up its own manufacturing capacity, there is increased competition from low-cost producers, and pressures build up which could affect both our terms of trade and the security of supply of our foodstuffs and key raw materials.

ELEMENTS OF AN INDUSTRIAL STRATEGY

7 It will be impossible to tackle these problems without action by all parties concerned, government, management, unions and the financial sector. We must therefore develop an agreed national strategy for industry on a long-term basis. Such a strategy must involve:

(i) the better co-ordination of policies affecting the efficiency of industry. This will require us to identify the industrial implications of the whole range of government policies. The feed-back of information from planning agreements with companies will be of particular value in this respect

(ii) the more effective use of the instruments of industrial policy and the deployment of financial assistance to industry. Both planning agreements and the NEB will be important here

(iii) ensuring that industry, both public and private, is able to earn sufficient profits on its investment to spur managements to expand and innovate and to provide them with the internal finance on which to base investment. Adequate sources of external funds are also vital: some will be provided through the National Enterprise Board and some through Finance for Industry, but it will also be essential that the market should be able to meet the needs of industry

(iv) a more effective manpower policy, including measures to provide a better supply of skilled manpower for growth industries and to cope with the human problems of people transferring from contracting to expanding industries. Training and retraining will be crucial here, both in coping with the problems of the present recession and in enabling people to meet the needs of a reorientated British industry. The Manpower Services Commission (MSC) and its agencies will have an important part in this

(v) the improvements in planning, both in industry and by government, which will flow from systematic and continuing tripartite discussion of the likely prospects of individual industries, allied to greater disclosure of information at company level, particularly, but not exclusively, in planning agreements.

Above all, we must get away from policies of confrontation, and work together in the national interest towards agreed objectives.

8 For its part, the government will have to continue maintaining a balance between economic and social objectives which often have conflicting implications. Nevertheless, the government intends to give greater weight, and more consistently than hitherto, to the need for increasing the national rate of growth through regenerating our industrial structure and improving efficiency. For the immediate future this will mean giving priority to industrial development over consumption or even our social objectives. There is no other way of developing the industrial base on which the government's whole programme of economic and social reform depends. The government will have to ensure the proper co-ordination of macro-economic and micro-economic policies since success will depend on a complex variety of factors needing support at national, industry and firm level. We recognise the need to maintain an adequate level of demand and employment if both sides of industry are to possess the confidence required to carry the necessary changes through.

9 The government must take the initiative in developing the industrial strategy,

but the main task of seeing that it brings higher productivity in British industry must fall on unions and management. Any major increases in productivity will require not only more investment better directed, but also improvements in working methods, including the reduction of overmanning and restrictive practices, and by transfer of workers into expanding sectors with a promising future. This will call for a major effort in training and retraining workers, together with effective co-ordination of the whole range of policies affecting the ease with which people can change jobs. The problems this poses will be for the Secretary of State for Employment to discuss with the NEDC and it will clearly call for wholehearted co-operation by the trade union movement at national and at plant level. The government favours a much greater involvement of work-people at all levels in industrial decision making. Similarly management will need to be alerted to opportunities at home and overseas and great efforts must be made to bring the level of efficiency and profitability of the poorer companies up towards that of the best. Thus at national level the TUC and the CBI will have an essential part to play together with the government, in evolving a common strategy for improving our industrial performance.

10 One response to the problem might be for the government to set in hand a new National Plan. The likelihood is that any plan which erected a single complete and mutually consistent set of industrial forecasts and targets would rapidly be falsified by events and have to be discarded. This would once again discredit the process of industrial planning in this country as did previous attempts, which failed largely because they were based on unsustainable economic assumptions, and paid too little attention to the constraints affecting individual industries and companies. On those occasions our national response to changes in circumstances which robbed us of early and visible success was to abandon the plan in question rather than to revise it and try again like the French or Japanese. Accordingly we find ourselves without any co-ordinated strategy to provide a consistent basis for government and industry to take their decisions.

11 This time a more flexible approach is proposed. We aim to provide a framework in which to consider the likely prospects of the most important sectors of industry over a period of five or more years ahead and to indicate their role in meeting our overall economic objectives. In developing this approach it will be essential to take full account of likely developments in world trade and in the competitive position of British industry relative to other countries: the effects of EEC membership, and in particular of the removal of internal tariffs, will be important factors. We hope this framework will be discussed extensively with both sides of industry as part of the development of the closer and more positive relationship between government and industry to which the government is committed in the White Paper on the Regeneration of British Industry (Cmnd 5710). The framework will need to be reviewed and if necessary adjusted, at regular intervals, to take account of changing circumstances. This would be related to what the government intends to do in planning agreements with major companies as well as to government planning of public expenditure and nationalised industry investment.

THE FRAMEWORK

12 The first step is the provision of a systematic statistical and analytical framework. Although this can ultimately be broadened to take account of other useful information, including work currently in hand in the National Economic

Development Office, we propose that the framework should initially rest on two main elements:

(i) An analysis of past performance of individual sectors of manufacturing industry based on a number of statistical indicators such as size, growth rate, trading performance, import content, growth of world demand and importance to other sectors. A key factor would be the competitiveness of the industry at home and abroad. This process will help identify the importance of individual sectors in achieving various objectives

(ii) the implications for different industries and sectors of alternative medium-term growth assumptions, using as a starting point the government's medium-term projection.

13 The government will make an initial assessment on the basis of this statistical framework, taking full account of a wide range of qualitative factors, such as the scope for improving on past performance, the potential for import substitution, the development of new technologies, the minimum economic size of plants, the security of future raw materials supplies (for example our self-sufficiency in energy in 1980), the impact of EEC membership and the scope for Community action, the emergence of new overseas competitors and industrial objectives and policies of other governments.

14 The aim will be to identify those sectors most important for achieving our economic objectives both for the government's purposes and for those of private industry. This will entail a sector-by-sector analysis to identify those which are likely to have most potential and those which may be expected to present problems. The most important industries will first be grouped in the following way:

—industries which, judging by past performance and current prospects, are intrinsically likely to be successful;

—industries which, though they fall short of the first category, have the potential for success if appropriate action is taken;

—industries whose performance (as in the case of component suppliers) is most important to the rest of industry.

It is of course clear that any industry can contain sub-sectors and individual firms whose prospects may be better or worse than the sector as a whole. Indeed some of the biggest disparities in performance at present are found within particular sectors rather than between them.

THE USE OF THE INDUSTRIAL FRAMEWORK

15 This analysis is not in itself an industrial strategy. It is a starting point for the development of the government's own industrial planning and a framework for discussion and action by the government and by both sides of industry at national, industry and company level. At each level, the objective must be to tackle the problems listed in paragraph 5 above, which lie at the root of our inadequate industrial performance since the war.

(i) *National Level*
16 At the national level, there is a wide range of government policies affecting industry. Industry will want closer consultation on medium-term macro-economic

prospects. We have made a start here by circulating to NEDC the main components of the government's medium-term projections and we shall be ready to consider ways of carrying this further to complement the discussion of sectoral prospects which will take place on a regular basis as indicated in paragraph 25 below.

17 For the government's policies to operate effectively government should be able to assess their effects on individual sectors of industry and take account of these effects in policy formation. The proposed medium-term industrial framework should help by providing an analysis of the factors which affect the prospects for various sectors, including the impact of possible changes in the government's general economic policies.

18 This sectoral framework can only be a part of the government's total strategy for industry. Quite apart from the policies for selective intervention (discussed further below) industry will want from the government an assurance that it accepts as a major objective of economic policy the ability of industry to earn a reasonable rate of return on capital. The government has made it clear that it accepts the importance of sustaining a vigorous, alert, responsible and profitable private sector of industry. It is equally important that public industry should be able to draw on retained surpluses for its own investments.

(ii) *Industry Level*

19 There will need to be extensive discussions of the analysis of industrial prospects with each of the industries identified within the groupings described in paragraph 14 above. The EDCs will have a great deal to contribute to this, and they will be able to draw upon the work they have been undertaking for the NEDO's medium-term industrial review. The structure and operation of the EDCs' machinery may have to be examined in the light of this new role. Other sectoral organisations such as trade associations may also contribute to the discussions.

20 Indicators which NEDO are preparing will be valuable at this stage in assessing the scope for improving performance within each sector. Publicly owned industries will have an important role to play in improving our overall industrial performance since it is essential that labour and capital resources should be efficiently used in the public as well as the private sector. Just as they will be brought into the planning agreements system, the nationalised industries will come within the scope of the strategic planning process. This will, for example, enable the long-term plans of the nationalised industries and their supplier industries to be related to each other and to the whole industrial framework. But since most of the nationalised industries are utilities rather than manufacturing industries, most of them are not, with the notable exception of steel, likely to feature in the grouping of paragraph 14.

21 These detailed discussions are likely to throw further light on possible constraints to improved performance and on the industrial implications of the government's economic projections and decisions. They might also lead to specific recommendations for action by companies, trade unions and government, although the selection of sectors will not imply any commitment that the government will necessarily intervene. However, the analytical framework should provide the government with a basis for determining priorities for action in specific areas of particular importance to the economy, within the inevitably limited resources available. This will contribute to the development of priorities for co-ordinated intervention and support not only by the government itself

but also by public agencies such as the NEB and the Manpower Services Commission.

### (iii) *Company Level*

22 The government will also discuss the industrial projections and their implications with individual companies, primarily though not exclusively in the context of planning agreements. It is the individual decisions taken by management and unions at the level of the firm which will in aggregate determine the UK's industrial performance. Planning agreement discussions should in due course provide a valuable means of influencing a significant proportion of the UK's manufacturing industry. While some firms will have opportunities which are not available to others in a given sector it would be the aim to improve the overall standard of a sector by raising the standard of average companies towards that of the best.

23 At the level of the firm, the government will seek to provide support where this is justified in individual cases—e.g. assistance for key investment projects— and the NEB will have a role in promoting changes in the management and organisation of individual companies as well as in securing the desired restructuring of a sector. In deciding whether individual companies merit support the government will have regard to its normal criteria, including the need to ensure that the company concerned is likely to be viable in the longer term. The framework and the development of a strategy will provide a comprehensive foundation for government policies both for companies in growth sectors and for companies in sectors with deteriorating prospects. It will also provide the framework within which the system of planning agreements will operate and a basis for the strategy of the NEB. The government's commitment to take full account of the agreed strategic framework and the more detailed knowledge of the government's thinking, which results from the process of providing it, should allow companies to plan ahead with greater confidence.

### (iv) *Procedure*

24 As has been made clear, the government views the development of an industrial strategy not as a single finite operation but as a continuing and evolving process, with arrangements for regular review after the initial discussions and agreement.

25 In a normal year the government envisages that the operation would move through three stages on the following lines. First, in the late summer, material would be put to the NEDC which would consist of three main parts:

(i) a paper setting out the main components of the government's medium-term projection

(ii) a paper identifying the most important sectors grouped in accordance with paragraph 14 and indicating the criteria which had been used for this purpose. As the 30 or so sectors would have been chosen primarily for their importance to the economy, it is unlikely they will change significantly from year to year, although as experience of the system develops it may be possible to add further criteria for selection. Nonetheless the government expects that the Council will wish to comment on the criteria chosen for any one year's review

(iii) separate annexes for each of the sectors listed. These would contain figures, where available, for the appropriate disaggregated part of the government's overall medium-term projections. They would also include a descriptive profile of the industry which would draw attention to its strong and weak points and in particular would attempt to identify areas where further trends were likely to differ from those in the past.

26 Second, subject to the Council's endorsement of the government's approach to the year's review, material in (iii) would be remitted to individual EDCs, or where no appropriate EDCs existed, to tripartite committees which would be set up *ad hoc* at least in the early stages. It would be in the EDCs, or *ad hoc* committees, that both sides of industry together with government would attempt to identify areas for improvement and possible action.

27 Third, the results of these discussions would be pulled together, perhaps by an official group representing the government, TUC, CBI and NEDO and submitted to the Council at about the turn of the year. This report would then form the basis for an important discussion by the Council on industrial policy in general, and in particular on areas highlighted for action and improvement, at a time of the year suitable for influencing the government's thinking on macro-economic policy.

28 None of this would in any way prevent or inhibit discussions in the Council or the EDCs at other times of the year on issues related to industrial strategy or the particular aspects of industrial performance. But it would provide a framework which would relate NEDC's main discussions on industrial matters to the government's own timetable. This would not preclude separate discussions with trade associations or similar bodies.

29 At this initial stage of development, the timetable for consultations must be treated flexibly. As explained above, the preparation of a sound statistical base entails a good deal of work, because much of it is breaking new ground and requires the application of considerable resources to develop techniques. However, the aim is to produce an experimental analysis for consideration by the Council early in the New Year. After discussion in the Council, the detailed examination at sectoral level could begin, although again at this stage it might need to be regarded as to some extent experimental. Progress might usefully be reviewed by the Council about the middle of next year when revised medium-term projections should become available. If we are to stick to this timetable the establishment of any additional groups that may be necessary will need to be set in hand quickly.

30 The government recognises that the proposals in this paper deal largely with questions of method and procedure and that the Council cannot take a final view about the merits of the new approach until it has had the further paper we hope will be ready by the turn of the year. They therefore invite the Council to agree that the further work that has been described should be undertaken and should be brought forward for discussion early in the New Year.

31 When these proposals have been put into practice, the government will be in a position to examine the problems of a wide range of industries and companies against a coherent framework. In playing its part in helping to deal with these problems the government will use the whole range of its powers. It will be able to frame its general economic policies so as to take account more systematically of the needs of industry. The NEB will be able to provide finance for companies in key sectors. Selective financial assistance will be used to encourage and assist viable projects and the sectoral discussions should enable appropriate schemes, like those already adopted for the ferrous foundries, machine tools, clothing, and

textile industries to be developed. Public purchasing policies will be used constructively in order to develop the export potential of appropriate industries. The MSC and its agencies will have a major role to play both in meeting the needs of growth sectors for suitable trained manpower and in easing the problems arising from industries shedding labour. All these instruments must come into play immediately wherever they are appropriate. The government is confident that they will make a still more valuable contribution to the necessary improvement of our industrial performance as the new strategy develops. But the main responsibilities will lie with both sides of industry in the sectors and firms involved.

# Short Reading List

In addition to the books mentioned in the text, the following general studies can be recommended:

Samuel Brittan, *Steering The Economy* (Penguin, Harmondsworth, 1964);
PEP, *Economic Planning and Policies in Britain, France and Germany* (London, 1968);
Andrew Shonfield, *Modern Capitalism* (RIIA/Oxford, 1965).
The annual *Economic Review* of the TUC provides a useful account of developments. Also worth reading, for an industrial analysis of the problems facing the UK in 1976 and their possible solutions, is the CBI's *The Road to Recovery*, published in November 1976.

# Index